From Under Zero to Financial Freedom

Decades of Building Wealth from Nothing: How I Raised Money Online, Then Made It Multiply Through Different Strategies

This book is born of resilience — the failures, disappointments, humiliations. It's about falling, getting back up, and d(you finally reach the shore of p(

It's not just another story. It's a journey of discovering what's right — even in the worst conditions, at the worst times, in the worst places, and often surrounded by the wrong people.

What you're about to read is the product of real struggle — forged through trial and error, fueled by persistence, and refined through clarity. These strategies are not theories. They worked for me, and if you follow them with commitment and consistency, they can work for you too.

This book exists to give you hope — to warm your heart. Because if someone like me — alone, broke, and seemingly powerless — could achieve what I have, then you can go even further. Chances are, you're starting from a better place than I ever did.

This isn't about secrets or shortcuts. There are no magic formulas. In the real world, wealth is built by doing the right simple things — repeatedly, and long enough to see results. That's what this book teaches: simple truths that most people ignore.

You don't need to be special. You don't need permission. You just need a real reason to begin — and a promise to yourself that you won't quit. You are here to start making money legitimately, to make that money work for you, and to build the path toward financial freedom. Then, you'll take it further — turning that freedom into lasting wealth, and eventually into total independence. Don't lose sight of this mission. Hold on to it until the day you've achieved it.

And no — this is not a "get rich quick" scheme. If something promises that, it's likely a scam. What you'll find here is the honest story of someone who started from far below zero and pushed through every obstacle. If you're holding this book, you're already ahead of where I began. That means you're closer to success than you may realize — as long as you're willing to do the work.

And finally, this book is the result of years of blood, sweat, and tears—of disappointments, renewed hope, and starting over again. Don't skip any part if you want it to work for you too. To truly benefit from it, you must first get to know me and establish a mental connection with me. Only then will you fully understand what I did—and be able to do the same to make it work for you.

Copyright Warning

© 2025 Vahid Chaychi. All rights reserved.

This book is protected under international copyright laws. No part of this publication may be reproduced, stored in a retrieval system, or transmitted in any form — electronic, mechanical, photocopying, recording, scanning, or otherwise — without the prior **written permission of the copyright holder**.

Translation Notice: The right to translate this book into other languages belongs exclusively to the copyright holder. **No individual, company, or organization is authorized to translate, adapt, or distribute this work in any language without official written permission.** Any unauthorized translation or distribution will be considered a serious infringement of copyright and will result in immediate legal action and prosecution under applicable laws.

Piracy, unauthorized reproduction, or distribution — whether in print, digital, or audio formats — is theft. The copyright holder actively monitors infringements and will pursue violators to the fullest extent of the law.

If you wish to request rights for translation, reproduction, or other permissions, please contact through WhatsApp: **Vahid Chaychi / Phone: +1 514 234 2261**

ISBN: 9798264767647

Disclaimer & Risk Warning

This book is for **educational and informational purposes only.** Nothing in these pages should be considered financial, legal, tax, or investment advice. The methods, strategies, and stories shared are based on personal experience, research, and opinion. Every reader's financial situation is unique, and results will always vary.

All investments carry **risk of loss.** Trading, stocks, real estate, cryptocurrencies, and other financial products mentioned here can be highly volatile and unpredictable. Past performance is not a guarantee of future results. You should **never invest money you cannot afford to lose.**

Before making any financial decisions, you are strongly encouraged to do your own due diligence, seek independent professional advice, and consult with qualified advisors such as licensed financial planners, accountants, or lawyers.

The author and publisher of this book accept **no liability** for any financial losses, damages, or outcomes that may occur from applying the information presented. You are fully responsible for your own choices, actions, and results.

By reading this book, you acknowledge and agree that you alone are responsible for your financial journey.

To my haters and enemies,

Thank you. You taught me one of the greatest lessons of my life — that in the end, I am the only one responsible for my own success. You showed me that not everyone will celebrate my victories, and that true freedom comes when I stop seeking approval and instead walk my journey alone.

Your doubts, insults, and attempts to hold me back became the fuel that pushed me forward. If it weren't for your resistance, I might never have discovered the strength, clarity, and resilience within me.

So, I am forever grateful. Every obstacle you placed in my path only sharpened my focus. Every attack reminded me to protect my peace. And every moment of your hate gave me one more reason to rise.

Because of you, I achieved the freedom I have today.
Thank you. Truly.

To my supporters and loved ones,

Thank you for standing beside me when the road was long, uncertain, and often lonely. Your faith in me became the light that guided me through the darkest moments, and your encouragement reminded me that no dream is too far when love surrounds it.

To my family, friends, and those who cheered me on — your kindness, patience, and belief in me were the anchors that kept me steady when storms came. Every smile, every word of encouragement, every moment of silent support gave me strength I didn't know I had.

To my father, who sacrificed his entire life for his country, his people, and his family without ever expecting anything in return — if it weren't for him, I would never be where I am today. I am forever in his debt.

I owe so much of my journey to you. Your love reminded me that success is not just about wealth or freedom — it's about having people who want to see you win.

Because of you, the journey has been brighter, and the destination, sweeter.
Thank you. From the depths of my heart.

Dear Reader,

First, let me thank you — deeply and sincerely — for choosing to read this book. Time is the most precious resource we have, and the fact that you are investing your time here humbles me. It tells me something important: you are serious about changing your life and taking control of your financial future. That commitment alone sets you apart from most people.

This book is not just a collection of ideas. It is the story of a journey — my journey — shaped by struggles, mistakes, lessons, and small victories that eventually built into something bigger. What you will read here is not theory or recycled advice. These are practical steps, proven principles, and real strategies that anyone — including you — can follow. My recommendation to you is simple but powerful:

1. **Read slowly and carefully.** Don't just skim through — reflect on each chapter.

2. **Stay consistent.** The magic is not in doing something once, but in doing it again and again until results compound.

3. **Trust the process.** At times, the journey may feel long or difficult. But remember, every great success starts with persistence through the early stages.

This is not just a book you finish and put back on the shelf. My hope is that it becomes a reference, a guide, and maybe even a companion on your journey toward financial freedom. Return to it when you need clarity, encouragement, or a reminder that freedom is possible for those who stay disciplined and patient.

Thank you again for giving me the privilege of walking this journey with you. May the lessons here spark courage, discipline, and vision in your life. And may your future self look back with gratitude on the moment you chose to begin — right here, right now.

With appreciation and belief in you,
Vahid Chaychi

CONTENTS

Introduction..9
Chapter 1 — Who I Am...12
Chapter 2 — Financial Freedom.......................................42
Chapter 3 — Make Money Online....................................50
Chapter 4 — Turning Earnings into Freedom...................162
Chapter 5 — Wisdom for the Journey..............................219

Introduction

I didn't start at zero. I started under it.

No money. No connections. No formal roadmap. Just a weak, self-assembled computer, a slow internet connection, and a relentless belief that somehow, some way, I could build something online—something real, something lasting, something that would change my life.

This book is not about overnight success. It's not about lucky breaks or secret shortcuts. It's about the truth — the long, uncertain, and often painful path I walked for over two decades, building an online business from the ground up, failing more times than I can count, and eventually finding a way not only to make money — but to *make that money work for me*.

Before we dive in, there's something important I need you to keep in mind:

As you read this book, you might come across parts that feel unrelated or slow. You may be tempted to skip ahead. But if you truly want this book to help you reach what I've reached — at the very least, financial freedom — I ask you to resist that urge.

You can't follow a recipe from the middle and expect it to work. You need to start from the beginning—even if some steps seem unnecessary. Maybe you're not starting from zero like I did. Perhaps you already have some money and are only interested in the strategies I share in the later chapters to grow your money.

That's fine — but **please be patient.** Read the book from the beginning, chapter by chapter, at least the first time. You need to know who I am, what I've been through, and — perhaps most importantly — **why you shouldn't blindly trust me**. Only when you understand the full picture will the strategies I share actually work for you.

After that, you're free to refer back to whichever parts you need — no need to reread the whole thing every time. But trust me when I say this: changing your life, making money, growing it, and reaching financial freedom isn't just about having the right roadmap. It's also about **building the right personality and mental strength** to follow it.

Without that, no strategy will work — no matter how good it is.

That's why so many incredibly talented people still struggle — while others, often seen as "ordinary," quietly succeed. The winners are those who first build the mindset they need. That's exactly what the early chapters of this book are meant to help you do.

Skip them, and the book will be useless to you. Read them, and it might just change your life. Rest assured, at the beginning of certain chapters, I'll let you know if I believe they may not be essential for some groups of readers. If you fall into one of those groups, feel free to skip that chapter. That's why, at least the first time, I ask you to trust the process and read the book from beginning to end.

Think of me as walking alongside you on this journey — as if I'm sitting right next to you, guiding you step by step.

Now...

If you've ever felt stuck, overwhelmed, or like you're starting too late or too far behind — this book is for you.

If you want to start making money to change your life and finally live the life you've always dreamed of — especially if you have no money, no idea how to start, and no clue where to begin — this book is for you.

If you've ever wanted to build something that makes money but didn't know where to start, this book is for you.

And if you've ever made money but didn't know how to grow or protect it — this book is definitely for you.

In these pages, I'll share:

- How I raised my first dollars when I had nothing but time and determination
- The strategies I used to build trust, generate revenue, and scale

- The approaches that allowed me to turn earned income into lasting wealth
- The *real lessons* — the ones no guru tells you — about failure, mental strength, and long-term success

I've kept nothing back. This is my story, my playbook, my failures, and my wins — all laid out so you can avoid the mistakes and fast-track your journey.

You don't need a perfect plan. You need persistence, honesty, and a willingness to start small and stay consistent.

Let's begin — right at the bottom — and I'll show you how I climbed from under zero to financial freedom.

Chapter 1
Who I Am — and Why This Journey Began

I was born in 1972 in a developing country in the Middle East — Iran. At that time, things were going well. The country was growing, and the government was focused on building a nation that could benefit both its people and, hopefully, the world.

My father was a government employee, and we lived in a beautiful house owned by the government, surrounded by trees, flowers, and the simple elegance of nature. Those were the best years of my life — a time when I learned to look at the sky, watch the sunset, listen to birds sing, smell the flowers, and breathe in the fresh air with joy.

The author, Vahid Chaychi (right), age 5, with his first friend in life by his side and his elder brother just behind him.

I remember many nights when, after lying in bed unable to sleep, I would get up, walk to the window, and gaze at the sky. The moon and stars captivated me. I would lose myself in their quiet brilliance, wondering what they truly were—and who might live among them. Hours would pass as I stood there, mesmerized by the mystery of the night sky. Looking back now, I realize I was in love from the very beginning—not with a person, but with something deeper: a love for knowing, for discovering the unknown. A love for nature and the endless, mysterious sky. A love for moving forward and reaching beyond, for flying freely through the realm of imagination. I loved to dream and weave stories—stories filled with wonder, questions, and the joy of answering them in beautiful, hopeful ways.

I can still recall vivid memories from as early as three or four years old — my unusually strong memory became both a source of strength and, at times, a burden. It gave me the gift of remembering details that proved invaluable throughout my life, yet it also made it harder to release painful moments from the past.

Even as a small child, I loved listening to classical music, especially while watching the sunset and hearing the birds settle in for the night. *"Air"* by Johann Sebastian Bach was my favorite. It made me feel like I was flying. Decades later, now in my fifties, it still feels just as fresh and moving every time I hear it.

Thanks to the television programming at the time, classical music was often broadcast before the official start of the daily schedule at 5 p.m. While the rest of my family disliked it, I would turn up the volume and let myself be swept away by its mesmerizing melodies.

Loving this kind of music from such an early age was unusual — and later in life, I realized it helped me understand something important about myself. I didn't quite fit in. It often felt like I belonged to a different world. That awareness helped me know who I truly was, and in many ways, it was a gift. But it also created problems.

Living among people who couldn't relate — and who sometimes even hated the things I loved — became my first real obstacle. It's a heavy burden to grow up in an environment where you're misunderstood for simply being yourself.

Even at those early ages, I began to notice that many of the people around me had deep emotional and psychological problems. Some were, quite literally, sick — not in body, but in mind and spirit. I could see it in their words and actions. They hurt themselves, and they hurt others — especially children. And I was one of those children.

The "good times" I mentioned earlier — the years of progress and peace — were relatively new. They had only begun a few years before I was born. Before that, the country had lived through hardship, oppression, and disasters that left deep scars on many people. Those scars turned some into bitter, cruel, and even destructive individuals.

Even after things improved, many of them couldn't — or wouldn't — change. It was as if their pain had become a part of them. And for a child like me — innocent, pure, and full of wonder — it was heartbreaking and terrifying to witness such darkness in the people around me.

Still, in spite of that, life in those early years remained beautiful in many ways. The country was growing. People were developing. A sense of well-being was beginning to spread, and many were learning how to live like decent human beings again.

But then… disaster struck.

Not just for the country — but for the whole world.

The 1979 Islamic Revolution

The people of Iran had lived under the shadow of extreme religious influence for over 1,400 years. Generations raised in that atmosphere were conditioned to believe in superstitions, reject reality, and suppress progress. Mental wounds ran deep — passed from one generation to the next — until ignoring facts and embracing fantasy became the norm.

When, at last, the door to a new era began to open — when the country started moving toward modernity, development, and scientific progress — many couldn't handle it. They saw advancement as a threat to their beliefs, and the government, which worked hard to uplift the nation, as an enemy of God (Allah). They didn't want a modern life. They wanted to go back — to live the way people lived 1,400 years ago.

Where I lived, I witnessed firsthand the government's efforts to modernize agriculture. New technologies were being introduced. Specialists were trained. My own father and two of his uncles were among them — part of the wave of progress. But to many people, these changes were seen as blasphemy. Progress was condemned as anti-religious. Knowledge was feared. Innovation was hated.

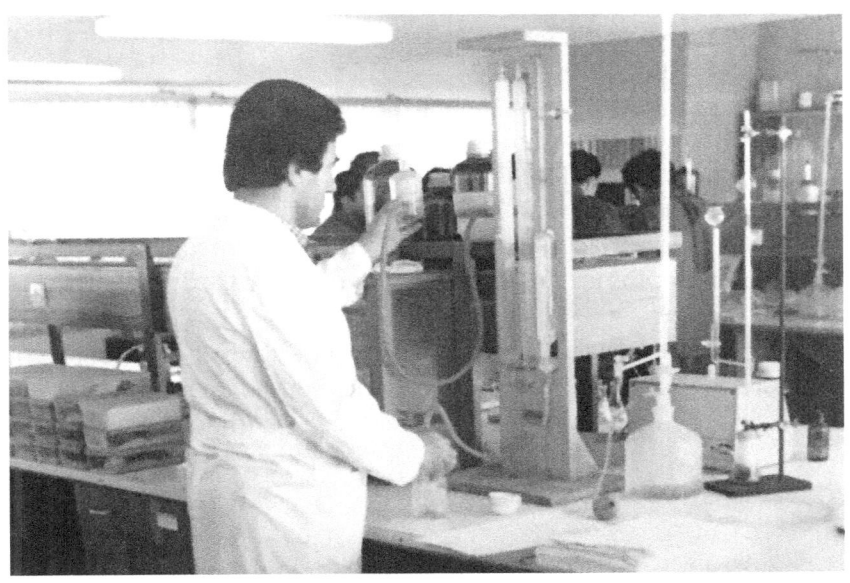

The author's father conducting research in a Soil Science Laboratory, 1977.

Eventually, the masses followed an extremist cleric named Khomeini — a man who was, in truth, an enemy of Iran's history, culture, and people. With his rise, the government was overthrown in 1979. Surprisingly, even the communist party — supported by the Soviet Union at the time — sided with the Islamic extremists against the government. Although communists and Islamists were ideologically opposed (one believed in God, the other rejected religion entirely), they shared a common goal: to eliminate the Shah and overthrow the government. Both groups, despite their differences, were enemies of Iran's progress — and in their temporary alliance, they succeeded in destroying everything the country had worked so hard to build.

It was a disaster — one that dragged the country back in time by 1,400 years.

Everything that had been built in the years prior was destroyed. A new dark era began — an era of repression, poverty, and fear. Torture, mass executions, war, censorship, discrimination, and blind obedience became the new normal. Blood flowed, voices were silenced, and dreams were shattered.

And I was only seven years old when it all began.

From 1979 until I left the country in 2004, life — for me and for most Iranians — was like living in hell.

Just one year after the revolution, in September 1980, a catastrophic war began. Iraq invaded Iran, and what followed was eight years of nonstop destruction. The war claimed hundreds of thousands of lives, left countless people disabled, and reduced entire cities, factories, and infrastructures to rubble. The country moved backward — fast.

Inflation began to soar during those years, and it never stopped. Even today, more than 45 years later, it continues to rise uncontrollably. For most people, having a normal, stable life became impossible.

But even that wasn't the worst part.

The true disaster came for those of us who had no connection to the new regime — the political and religious system that rose from the ashes of the revolution. If you weren't part of them, you were considered an outsider... an enemy. You had no rights. No voice. No protection. No place.

It was a true example of fascism — no different from what Hitler did to Jews and other minorities. The only difference was, we weren't even a minority. We were simply people who didn't belong to the revolution.

And for that, we were punished.

You had only three options:

Live under the regime and suffer, knowing you had no future — even if you earned the highest degrees.

Leave the country, if you could.

Or join the Islamic regime and become one of those destroying the nation from within.

There was no fourth choice.

Many of my friends and relatives escaped the country as soon as they could. But for me, that wasn't an option. I stayed — and continued my studies under that unbearable condition. I completed high school and enrolled in university, even though I knew deep down that I was wasting my time. No matter how much I achieved, I couldn't go anywhere meaningful under that system.

Looking back now, I often wish I had been brave enough to run — to leave right after getting my high school diploma. Instead, I went on to earn a master's degree. And guess what? It still didn't matter. I wasn't one of "them." I had no connections. So I was left with no choice but to complete the mandatory military service at the age of 26.

Many of my classmates and peers had ties to the regime. They bought their way out of military service and went straight into well-paying jobs. But for me, those years were the darkest of my life. The pressure I felt… the burden on my shoulders… I still can't fully describe it.

And worst of all, after decades of living under such a broken system, the people had changed. They had become enemies of each other. Mistrust poisoned everything. Friends betrayed friends. Relatives hurt each other. No one was safe. You couldn't trust anyone — not even those closest to you. And yes, I was hurt, more than once, by the very people I thought I could rely on.

I knew then that I had no choice but to leave. But I didn't want to escape illegally. I wanted to do it the right way. That meant finishing my military service, getting a passport, and applying for immigration to a country like Canada or Australia.

So, that's what I did.

After completing my service, I applied to immigrate to Canada in the year 2000. I thought I'd be gone within a couple of years.

But then, disaster struck again.

September 11, 2001.

The attacks brought everything to a halt — including immigration processing. My application sat frozen for more than two years.

Can you imagine that?

Can you even begin to understand what it feels like to live through what I lived through?

No one should have to experience what I did.

The Islamic Regime — A Disgrace to Humanity

In Iran, people are ruled by a regime obsessed with developing nuclear weapons — not to defend the country or improve lives, but to tighten its grip on power and secure its own survival. At the same time, it demands that citizens live as if it were still 1,400 years ago.

So far, the regime has spent over $2 trillion of the nation's budget pursuing its nuclear ambitions, while the people have become increasingly impoverished and hopeless. Rates of mental illness, suicide, and both physical and psychological disorders have skyrocketed. Diseases that were once eradicated have returned. In some regions, there aren't even enough vaccines for children.

And yet, the regime continues to insist that everything is fine — because, in their own words, *"We work for Islam, not for the people."*

It doesn't matter how talented or hardworking you are. If you're not one of them, you have no future. No opportunity. No recognition. Meanwhile, the least competent individuals are elevated to the highest positions — not for their merit or skill, but for their loyalty to the regime.

It's a system built on exclusion, oppression, and deception — and it remains one of the greatest disgraces to humanity in our time.

During the 25 years I lived under its shadow, I witnessed horrors no human being should ever see.

I saw public tortures and executions with my own eyes. I heard the cries of families whose loved ones had been arrested or killed — not for any crime, but for having a belief, reading a forbidden book, or simply carrying a political leaflet in their pocket.

I saw teenagers — some as young as 18, or even younger — raped, tortured, and left to die, simply for belonging to a political group the regime didn't like. Their only "crime" was daring to think differently — or hope for something better.

I still remember the grave of a young man and his pregnant wife — both executed by the regime. They were buried in secret, in the garden of the man's father, because the authorities declared them infidels, unworthy of burial in public cemeteries.

I saw a man whose four fingers were cut off as punishment for stealing a small amount of money. At the same time, I saw regime loyalists steal billions — confiscating hundreds of thousands of hectares of land left behind by those who had fled the country to avoid imprisonment or death. These criminals lived safely, comfortably, and shamelessly enjoyed what they had stolen.

One of them — a relative of mine — doesn't even have a high school diploma. Yet the regime's state-run television introduced him as an "engineer" and a "pioneer of entrepreneurship," simply because he supports the regime.

That's how the system works: support the regime, and you can do whatever you want — no matter how immoral, corrupt, or criminal.

I saw highly educated people — with advanced degrees and years of study — forced to work as drivers or construction laborers just to survive. Their only "fault" was refusing to conform to the regime's ideology. Meanwhile, those who served the regime were rewarded with power, wealth, and even honorary doctorate degrees — regardless of their qualifications.

These were the tragedies that became normal under the Islamic regime.

And I lived with them — every day — for 25 years.

Is that all?

No — not even close.

Living under such a system doesn't just destroy institutions and infrastructure. It breaks people from the inside. It makes everyone unstable. Distrust, fear, and desperation take over, and people slowly become enemies of one another — a condition the Islamic regime exploits to maintain control.

You get hurt by everyone — even those closest to you. Anyone who comes near is either trying to take advantage of you, or will eventually betray you. Trust becomes dangerous. I've seen fathers betray their own children and grandchildren for money. They may not kill you, but they will not hesitate to make you as miserable as possible if it serves their interests.

In such an environment, keeping your mental and emotional balance becomes nearly impossible.

Did I Get Hurt Too?

Yes — deeply.

How could anyone live in such an environment and not get hurt? I wasn't made of stone or iron. I was a human being, surrounded by people who had been twisted and darkened by the conditions around them.

Not only did I witness terrible things — people tortured, imprisoned, even killed — but **I was also hurt myself**. Not by strangers alone, but by people both near and far. Even after I grew up and started climbing the ladder of progress, trying to build a better life for myself, I faced an even more bitter truth:

Many of those closest to me wanted me to stay crushed.

They didn't want to see me rise. And when they did see it — when they saw I was going up — their response wasn't support or celebration. It was **hostility, ridicule, and belittling**.

I'll never forget the moment I moved to Canada and officially registered my company. I was proud. I had worked hard to get there. But instead of congratulations from the people I thought would be the happiest for me, I was met with mockery.

That hurt more than I can describe.

But you've heard the saying: *"What doesn't kill you makes you stronger."*
Or how the **lotus**, one of the most beautiful flowers, grows from the **muddiest marshes**.
Or that a **diamond** is just a rough stone — until it's cut and polished under pressure.

The truth is: **you can't rise if you're always bleeding from your past**. You have to stop serving those who don't deserve you. You have to stop explaining yourself to people who secretly hope you'll fail. You have to **recognize toxic patterns**, protect your energy, and heal your wounds.

Only then can you rise — like an eagle soaring toward the sky.

In an environment like the one I came from, this is the only real choice: **Heal and grow — or remain wounded and watch your future slip away.**

Physical Illnesses

Living under such harsh conditions took a toll on me physically, not just emotionally. I developed several health problems at a young age.

When I was just 9 years old, I was diagnosed with chronic lung disease — something that took a very long time to heal. There were moments when I couldn't breathe at all. I still remember a few terrifying times when my breathing completely stopped, and everything around me went dark. I came frighteningly close to death. And yet — somehow — after a short while, I would open my eyes again and realize I was still alive.

I also developed kidney problems, which I continue to deal with to this day. On top of that, I suffered from migraines since childhood —

intense headaches that would leave me nearly unconscious at times. Although this condition is more controlled now, it's still something I live with.

Sometimes, when I think about how I managed to survive all of this — the pain, the fear, the illnesses — I'm stunned. And yet, here I am. I stayed alive. And at the age of 54, I'm writing this book — sharing my story with you.

Innocence

What I've been through has taught me something powerful: **all children are born kind, innocent, caring, loving, and emotionally whole.** They arrive in this world with pure hearts and open minds. They love unconditionally. They don't wish harm on anyone.

But something tragic often happens — not because of who they are, but because of where they grow up.
It's the environment, and the wounded people around them, that slowly cloud their pure, shining minds and turn that light into confusion, fear, and sometimes darkness.

Yet, despite all that, **their pure soul is never truly lost.**
It remains, deep inside — untouched and waiting.
If a person awakens early enough in life, they can dust off the darkness, clear the confusion, and return to the beautiful, original self they were born as.

That is our responsibility — to ourselves, and to the generations that follow.
We must heal, grow, and refuse to pass our pain forward.

If we do this, humanity will evolve. Life will get better.
But if we don't, the malice will only grow — and in time, it will ruin everything.

Development of Talents

Some of the sweetest memories of my childhood are from the days my father took me to work with him. Even before I started school, those visits gave me the precious opportunity to explore a modern laboratory—an experience that would shape the rest of my life.

It was there, surrounded by beakers, tubes, analytical scales, and mysterious machines, that I was first introduced to the wonders of chemistry. I learned about acids and bases and how they interacted with metals and stones. I saw precise analytical scales in action and marveled at the various instruments and glassware used in experiments. For the first time, I looked through a microscope and discovered a hidden universe—tiny, colorful, and more intricate than anything I had seen with the naked eye.

I even learned that glass tubes and vessels could be shaped by heating and bending, a simple act that felt like magic to a child. I encountered tools like the pH meter and grasped the meaning of acidic, basic, and neutral substances. Remarkably, I absorbed all of this before I could even read or write.

Those early experiences didn't just teach me science—they transformed how I saw the world. They opened my mind, sparked my curiosity, and ignited a lifelong passion for learning, creating, and understanding. From that point on, the world was no longer ordinary—it was a place of wonder, filled with hidden truths waiting to be discovered.

When I was nine years old, my father opened a small toy and baby clothing store as a side hustle. That summer, he gave me a chance to run my own little business too. I stood in front of his shop as a peddler, selling plastic sandals and handmade wooden artwork. To my father's surprise, there were days when my small stand made more sales than his entire store. That was the very first time I tasted the thrill of business and understood what it meant to earn money on my own.

As I grew older, I took on other summer jobs that shaped my work ethic and character. I worked in a mechanic's shop, where I was sometimes trusted to manage the store entirely on my own, even at a young age. In another summer, I worked as a welder on a construction project. Each of these experiences taught me resilience, responsibility, and the value of combining knowledge with hands-on practice.

These lessons never left me. They became part of who I am — a foundation of practicality that has guided me through every step of my journey. No matter how much knowledge or expertise I later gained, it was always strengthened and grounded by those early experiences of rolling up my sleeves and working hard.

Later, during my university years, I worked part-time in medical laboratories, particularly in the microbiology and biochemistry departments. I also pushed myself further by enrolling in additional training courses on advanced techniques. These included molecular genetics, electron microscopy, and several other specialized areas. Looking back now, I sometimes amaze even myself with how much I did, how much I learned, and how hungry I was for knowledge at such a young age.

Those years taught me discipline, curiosity, and the power of deep learning — qualities that would later carry over into business and investing. Every hour I spent in those labs and training rooms added another layer of resilience and skill, preparing me for challenges I couldn't yet see but would eventually face on my journey toward freedom.

Immigration to Canada

In 2004, I finally received my immigration visa to Canada. That moment brought a wave of hope and happiness into my life — because after 25 years, I was finally escaping the hell created by the Islamic regime and the toxic environment that surrounded it.

It felt like being released from solitary confinement — a prison of darkness, fear, torture, and constant disappointment. For the first time in decades, I could breathe.

My original plan was to continue my education and pursue a PhD in medical virology or molecular genetics, as I already held a Master's degree in Medical Virology. After becoming a landed immigrant in 2004, I took the TOEFL exam and applied to PhD programs at the University of Toronto and the University of Guelph. I was accepted by both. But I never enrolled.

Instead, I chose to keep working on my business—the very journey this book is about. Had I taken the academic path, you wouldn't be reading this now. This book would never have been written.

Even before I set foot on Canadian soil—while I was still in Iran—I had already begun laying the foundation for something entirely different: a business that would shape the rest of my life.

And this is where the fun part begins.

What followed was a long road of trial and error — of failures, mistakes, persistence, and eventual success. I'll take you deep into how I built that business, step by step, because it's something you can do too.

This is where the money hopefully begins to flow into your life — but more importantly, it's where you learn how to make that money work for you. I'll explain the exact strategies I used to grow my income and build lasting wealth — strategies you can follow, no matter where you are starting from.

Why Business — and Not Continuing My Education

Since I couldn't find a job related to my academic background—largely because it required strong connections and support I simply didn't have—I turned to the skills I had developed on my own: computer literacy. I had been using those skills to make a living for several years before I ever immigrated to Canada.

When I began my MSc degree in 1996, I knew absolutely nothing about computers—not even how to turn one on. The university library was the first place I encountered them. Like most students at the time, I relied on the staff to help me search for journals and articles. But something shifted quickly.

I was fortunate to have access to a computer in the department where I worked on my research projects. That opportunity became the spark. Within months, I went from being a complete novice to someone others turned to for help. When the library's computers had issues and the technicians weren't available, I was the one they called. The newbie had become the go-to expert in a surprisingly short time.

That was the beginning of a lifelong journey. I started taking courses in programming, web development, and other computer-related fields. What began as a necessity slowly turned into a passion—and eventually, a career. That journey has now spanned nearly 30 years, and it's still continuing.

From Skills to Sales — The Turning Point

Conan O'Brien once said, *"Work hard, be kind, and amazing things will happen."*
I've found that to be absolutely true.

You just need to choose a niche and become an expert in it. That doesn't happen without consistent hard work and learning. You won't see great results at the beginning — but if you keep going, as Conan says, amazing things will happen.

A few years before I immigrated to Canada — while I was working as a data analyst, computer expert, web developer, and more, just to make ends meet — an ad in a newspaper caught my attention. It mentioned something I had never seriously considered: the possibility of becoming an online salesman.

Until then, I believed I could only use my computer and internet skills for freelance projects — getting hired to build websites, assemble computers, fix software problems, or develop custom tools. I had no idea that I could combine what I already knew with marketing and generate actual sales.

That ad opened a new world to me. It simply said: **"Become an Online Salesman."**
Something clicked.

I signed up for the course, and that was the beginning of a new journey — a journey that would eventually change everything.

By the time I landed in Canada, that journey had already paid off. I had made enough money through my online efforts to buy a house in a good neighborhood, a brand-new car, and everything else I needed to begin a new life in a new country.

It didn't happen overnight. In fact, it took me two full years of trial and error just to earn my first five dollars online. But I didn't give up. And within a year of that tiny start, those five dollars turned into thousands in monthly income.

The Hidden Gift in a Crisis

Now, looking back, I realize that the event which delayed my immigration by more than two years turned out to be a hidden blessing for me personally. At the time, it felt like another setback. But in truth, it gave me something invaluable: **time to reflect on my future and redefine my path.**

Up until then, I thought my only option was to continue my education, earn a PhD, and then find a job. That meant years of studying, taking on debt, and hoping to land a position or research project that might pay the bills. But deep down, that life didn't excite me. It didn't feel like the future I truly wanted. Still, it seemed like the only logical path available.

But the long wait for my immigration visa — which felt bitter and frustrating at the time — gave me the unexpected chance to learn new skills and prepare in ways that ultimately placed me far ahead of where I would have been otherwise. By the time I set foot in Canada, I wasn't starting at the bottom. I was already equipped with tools, knowledge, and experience that put me in a stronger position than most.

The lesson? There is **opportunity in every crisis** — if you're willing to look for it.
Even the darkest moments can become turning points. You just have to shift your perspective and stop focusing only on the negative. Whether or not you believe that everything happens for a reason, the truth is: **you can learn something from everything that happens — good or bad — and find doors that would otherwise remain closed.**

So now you understand why I chose not to enroll in a PhD program and instead focused on building my business. I still believe it was the right decision. But honestly, even if I had chosen the academic route, I believe I would have succeeded there too — because I've learned something that applies to every area of life:

It doesn't matter what you do — what matters is how well you do it.

This isn't about perfectionism. It's about commitment. If you want great results, you have to give your best in whatever you pursue.

Don't Wait for Help — Do It on Your Own

The only person who ever truly helped me was my father. He supported me through my education and paid for my immigration to Canada. He's the one person I genuinely consider myself indebted to.

Everyone else? They were either indifferent or outright against everything I tried to do.

Why? As I've explained before, living under that regime, in that broken environment, turned people into something they were never meant to be. Everyone was wounded in some way—mentally, emotionally, or spiritually. It was a world full of distrust, fear, and pain. People weren't able to help because they were too busy trying to survive themselves.

If you're lucky enough to have kind, supportive people around you — ask for their help, and be grateful. But if you don't, that's okay too. **Do it on your own.**

I've seen people who didn't even have the support of their own parents—and still, they rose. They struggled. They fought. And they flourished.

Always remember this: **No one is obligated to help you.** And the conditions you're waiting for — the "perfect moment," the "ideal circumstances" — they may never come.

So don't wait. Don't hope. Don't beg.

Start now. Do what you can with what you have. And whatever you do — don't give up.

The Initial Setup

After completing the "Become an Online Salesman" course, I made the decision to start earning money through the Internet. To do that, I needed two things: a computer and an internet connection.

From day one, my approach was simple — **get the maximum results with the minimum cost**. That mindset has stayed with me ever since. While many people rush to buy the most expensive equipment when starting a business, I did the opposite.

I assembled a desktop computer myself, piece by piece, buying every component second-hand. The only parts I allowed myself to buy new were the monitor and keyboard — and even those were the cheapest I could find at the time. In the end, the entire setup cost me less than $100, yet it became one of my greatest tools for learning, building, and moving forward.

The internet connection I used in Iran was dial-up — slow, unreliable, and nothing close to today's standards. But it worked. And more importantly, **I worked.**

I ended up making hundreds of thousands of dollars with that cheap computer and the slow dial-up internet. Looking back, it proved once again that what Jim Rohn famously said is absolutely true: *"If you want to do something, you will find a way. If you don't, you will find an excuse."* My computer wasn't powerful, my internet was painfully slow, and I didn't have the comfort or resources most people think are necessary to succeed. But I had the will, the drive, and the discipline. That was enough to turn a $100 setup into the foundation of my financial freedom.

The first computer I ever owned—assembled piece by piece by myself in 2001.

Later, when I moved to Canada, I upgraded to a high-speed DSL connection. But surprisingly, it didn't make much of a difference in terms of my output — because I was just as committed when I had almost nothing. I didn't wait for perfect conditions. I just got to work.

Not having the best tools or ideal conditions can be a barrier — but only for those who are looking for one. If you're serious, you'll either **find a way** or **build one.**

Starting the First Online Business

The "Become an Online Salesman" course taught me something that changed everything: you could sell products online — and even if you didn't have your own product (which I didn't at the time), you could sell other people's products as an **affiliate** and earn commissions.

That was the perfect starting point for me.

I had already learned how to develop websites, but launching one in Iran was nearly impossible. To start a website, you need to register a domain and buy hosting — both of which require online payment. But in Iran, that was a major obstacle. There were no internationally accepted credit cards or valid online payment methods available to us at the time.

Still, as I've said before: **when you're serious about doing something, you'll find a way — no obstacle can stop you.**

After a long search, I discovered that there was a **Master Debit card** managed from the United Arab Emirates. I could buy one, load it with money, and use it to make online payments. It was expensive to get and fund, but I did it anyway — because I had made up my mind.

With that card, I was finally able to:

- Register my first domain
- Purchase hosting
- Launch my first website
- Add content and start working

I also joined a well-known affiliate program, which required a membership fee that I paid using the Master Debit card. Thankfully, international sanctions against Iran were not yet as strict at that time, and companies still accepted members from Iran. That was a stroke of luck. If I hadn't been able to join then, I would have had to wait until I moved to Canada.

But I didn't have to wait.

I joined. I worked. I built several websites — **all while I was still in Iran.**
Since I couldn't receive payments inside the country (foreign checks couldn't be cashed in Iran), I set my affiliate accounts to **accumulate earnings** until I could finally withdraw the money after immigrating.

Did I make money right away?

No.

It took me **two years** of hard work, trial and error, setbacks, frustration, and persistence to earn my **first commission — just five dollars.**

So why didn't I give up, like most people do? Why didn't I throw in the towel and say, "I tried, but it didn't work"?

Because I **refused to quit.**

Because I was willing to do whatever it took.

Because I understood that results don't come instantly — but they do come, eventually.

Because I told myself: *if others can do it, I can too.*

Because my life had taught me that **no one would save me — I had to save myself.**

Because even when nothing looked promising, I held on to hope.

Because I had been wounded, disappointed, and broken… and I wanted to rise, to change my life, and to make a difference.

The Key

The key to success — especially when you're starting something new — is this:

Keep going.

Keep going even when you see no results.
Keep going even when the results are disappointing.
Keep going even when things are going well.

Because that's exactly where most people stop — and lose everything they've worked for.

But persistence alone isn't enough. As Einstein famously said:

"Insanity is doing the same thing over and over and expecting different results."

You can't just repeat the same mistakes and expect a miracle. Yes, you must work harder when results aren't showing — but at the same time, you must **analyze**, **adjust**, and **refine your approach**.

If one method doesn't work — and you've truly given it a fair chance — don't give up. **Change your method. Test a new path. Adjust your strategy. Try again.**

Do this as many times as it takes — because that's exactly what every successful person in history has done. Otherwise, we wouldn't know their names today.

When someone told Thomas Edison that he had failed 10,000 times in his quest to invent the light bulb, he replied:

"I have not failed. I've just found 10,000 ways that won't work."

That mindset is what separates those who succeed from those who give up.
You only fail when you quit.

The beginning is always the steepest part of the climb.
There are no rewards, only effort. No applause, just silence.

But if you **resist**, **persist**, and **keep pushing**, you will hit the **lift-off point** — that magical place where everything speeds up, and the results finally begin to multiply. And that's exactly what happened to me.

As I mentioned, it took me two long years of trial, error, struggle, and spending both time and money — just to earn my first **five dollars**.

That's the difficult part of the story.

But here's the part I want you to remember:

Once I figured out what to focus on — once I had the right strategy in place — my income **skyrocketed**.

In just **about a year** after making that first $5, I was earning between **$20,000 and $27,000 USD per month** from my websites and affiliate programs.

Yes — **per month**.

I continued accumulating my affiliate income while still in Iran, letting it grow inside my accounts. After several years of working and waiting, I finally received my immigration approval. As part of the process, I had to open a Canadian bank account. My immigration consultant in Canada helped arrange it after my interview was successfully completed.

Once the account was active, I contacted the affiliate companies and asked them to wire my accumulated earnings directly to my new Canadian account. Thankfully, **most of them agreed** and transferred the funds without any issues. A few companies, however, only paid via physical checks — so I had to continue letting that income accumulate until I could physically arrive in Canada and cash them.

And that's how this so-called poor, helpless, and underestimated guy — who had once been stuck under impossible conditions — was able to **buy a house**, a **brand-new car**, and everything he needed **immediately after immigrating to Canada**.

At a time when most new immigrants are struggling to find a survival job just to cover rent and basic expenses, I had already built a foundation for financial independence.

Your attitude determines your altitude.
Work hard. Be kind. **Amazing things will happen.**

People Were Amazed

I quickly rose through the ranks to become the **top-performing affiliate** for many companies — even outshining seasoned veterans from places like the United States. For several months in a row, I held top positions on leaderboards, surprising even the most experienced marketers.

Many people were impressed and offered kind words of praise and encouragement.

Of course, not everyone was kind. A few individuals — very rare, but still memorable — mocked me for my poor writing skills in articles and emails. Others made fun of my appearance, especially the **mustache** I had at the time. ☺

But none of that mattered. Because I was winning — and I knew I was just getting started.

I think this is a good time to say how **deeply grateful** I am to the great country of the **United States of America** — and to the many **amazing and outstanding companies** I worked with there, including the **cyber giants like Google**.

Without them, I would never have achieved what I did online. They gave me the platform, the tools, and the opportunity to build something meaningful from nothing.

And of course, none of this would have been possible if I hadn't moved to **Canada** — a country that welcomed me with open arms. **Canada's freedom, its supportive system, and its excellent banking infrastructure** allowed me to finally unlock the doors I had been knocking on for years.

I will be forever thankful to these two modern nations — They were **kinder to me than most people in my own life**.

Those Who Inspired Me the Most

The journey to success requires **fuel** — something to keep you going when times get tough. Most of the time, you are your own primary source of energy and motivation. In fact, in many cases — as it was for me — the people around you won't give you energy or encouragement. Instead, they'll **drain your energy** with cold words, naysaying, and negativity.

You must be strong enough to **ignore them** — and move forward even stronger.

However, having **role models and legends** to follow can make a huge difference. Their lives, their stories, and the wisdom they've left behind can not only change your life but also help you **find the right direction** when you're about to give up or when you've taken the wrong path.

In my life, I've had a few key legends to follow — and some of their quotes have **saved me from defeat** more than once.

One of the most important figures for me is **Albert Einstein**. He left behind many remarkable quotes that can guide you through nearly every challenge in life. The one that has helped me the most — and reminds me to adjust my approach when I'm not getting results — is his famous quote on insanity:

"Insanity is doing the same thing over and over and expecting different results."

Most people make this mistake. When they don't get results, they **keep doing the same thing**, hoping that this time, somehow, the outcome will be different. But as Einstein says, that's insanity.

This doesn't mean you should constantly abandon your course. **It means that when you've tried something long enough and it's not working, you need to pause — analyze — refine — and then keep going with a better method.**

Always keep this quote in mind. It can save you years of wasted effort.

One of Einstein's other **game-changing quotes** is:

"We cannot solve our problems with the same thinking we used when we created them."

This quote has helped me countless times when I found myself stuck with a problem. It's a simple but powerful truth: **if your current level of thinking created the problem, that same level of thinking will not solve it.**

To fix it, you must **elevate your thinking** — or, as I like to say, reach a **higher level of consciousness**. Otherwise, not only will you fail to solve the problem, but you may actually make it worse.

And here's the key: **if you can't yet reach that higher level of thinking yourself, don't let your ego get in the way.** Seek out the wisdom of those who are already operating on that higher level — the **experts, mentors, and wise minds** who can guide you through it.

Sometimes, the fastest way to solve a problem is to borrow the vision of someone who already sees what you can't.

Another powerful quote from Einstein is about **understanding the process before taking action**:

"If you can't explain it simply, you don't understand it well enough."

This quote has always reminded me that before you start doing something, you must **know exactly what you're doing** — and understand it deeply. Yet, most people ignore this step. They jump into a new business or project without even grasping what it truly involves.

I've seen many people start businesses they know almost nothing about. For example, someone decides to become a builder just because they've heard that builders make good money. But when you ask them about the process, they can't even explain the basics — they don't understand the steps, the risks, or the industry.

How can anyone expect to succeed at something they don't even understand well enough to explain in simple terms?

The path is clear:

1. **Research and investigate first.**
2. **Collect information and learn.**
3. **Analyze the conditions.**
4. **Make a solid plan.**
5. **Only then, start taking action.**

Without understanding and planning, action is just a blind gamble.

The last quote from Einstein that I must share here is about **simplicity**, a principle he applied even in his groundbreaking scientific work:

"Everything should be made as simple as possible, but not simpler."

All problems — whether they are in mathematics, physics, business, or life — seem complicated at first. But it's your job to **simplify them** before you begin solving them.

If a process looks overly complex and difficult to understand, don't rush into it. **Break it down into clear, manageable steps** — and only then start working on it. This is a habit I've developed over the years, and it has helped me in every area of life and business.

However, the second part of the quote — *"but not simpler"* — is just as important.
While simplicity is key, oversimplifying a process can lead to **underestimating the work involved** and failing to take it seriously. The challenge is to simplify **without losing the essence** of what truly needs to be done.

There are two other legends I have followed my whole life — and I will continue to follow them. One of them is a pioneer who helped shape modern America with his engineering brilliance and entrepreneurial vision.

One of his quotes has always inspired me, keeping my thoughts positive and strengthening my belief that I can achieve whatever I set my mind to:

"Whether you think you can, or you think you can't – you're right."

This simple statement holds incredible power.
Your life and future depend on how you think about yourself.

If you believe wealth and success are not meant for you, then you're right — they never will be. But if you believe that you *can* achieve wealth and success — because you see that others have done it, and you know there's no reason you can't do it too, perhaps even better — then you will find the path to make it real.

You are what you think.
The quality of your life is a direct reflection of the quality of your thoughts.

The Last — and Most Important — Legend

The last, but perhaps the most important legend in my life, is **Warren Buffett** — someone I study, admire, and learn from **every single day**. To me, he represents the ultimate example of **wisdom, patience, discipline, and stability** — qualities that are essential for success in any area of life.

I will talk about Warren Buffett more in the upcoming chapters, especially when we discuss how to make your **money work for you** — which is the most critical step toward financial freedom (explained in Chapter 2).

But before we move forward, here is one of his quotes that you must memorize and remind yourself of **every single day** until you achieve it:

"If you don't find a way to make money while you sleep, you will work until you die."

This single quote can **change your life** — if you let it.
It perfectly captures the difference between struggling to survive paycheck to paycheck and living a life of comfort, happiness, and early freedom.

It highlights the **vital importance of building multiple streams of income — especially passive income**, which is the foundation of true financial freedom. This will be one of the **core lessons of this book**, and I will dive deep into it in the chapters ahead.

Just look around you. How many elderly people do you see who are still forced to work just to survive?
Many don't even have a home of their own. Why?

Because **nobody ever taught them** that without building passive income — without creating a way to "make money while you sleep" — they would be condemned to work until their final day. And sadly, that's exactly what they are doing: **working until they die**, simply because they have no choice.

In the next chapter, I will share more on this topic — including the inspiring story of a **cleaning lady** who, despite her modest job, had the wisdom and foresight to realize that she couldn't keep working forever. She found a way to make her money work for her — and she succeeded.

This is the **main mission of this book**, and it should be **your mission too**:
Learn how to make money, then learn how to **make your money make more money for you** until you reach financial freedom.

Get ready to do it.
And don't stop until you achieve it — **no matter what.**

Bottom Line

Chapter One may have felt more like a second introduction — and that's exactly what it was. It explained how I lived, how I struggled, and how I eventually discovered the world of online business and started making money.

In the chapters ahead, I'll walk you through the exact process in more detail. But even more importantly, I'll introduce you to a critical step that most people overlook on their path to financial freedom — **the step that comes after you start making money**:

You must learn how to make your money work for you.

Without this step, you'll never become financially free — no matter how much you earn from your business. That's because income from a business is **active income**. And active income always requires your time and effort.

If you're starting from zero — or like me, from *under* zero — your first job is to work hard, build something, and earn money. That's the first stage. But once you've accumulated enough capital, you must shift your focus. You must move from **hard work** to **smart work**.

That's the true key to freedom.

In the next chapters, I'll show you:

- How I built my online business step by step
- How I scaled it into consistent income
- And how I transitioned from just making money to creating true financial freedom

I strongly recommend that you **don't skip any chapters** — at least on your first read. Even if something doesn't seem relevant at first glance, I promise you'll discover valuable insights that can change the way you think about money, wealth, and freedom.

In the next chapter, I'll explain the **real meaning of financial freedom**, how it differs from simple wealth, and what you need to do to live as a financially free person — so you can enjoy life without having to work forever.

Thank you for reading this far.
Now let's begin the journey to true freedom.

Thank you! I love you! ♥

Chapter 2
Financial Freedom

This chapter may completely change the way you think about wealth — and even about life itself. That's why I encourage you to read it carefully. It will help you set meaningful, lasting goals for the rest of your journey.

Most people want to become rich. Even if they can't achieve real wealth, they still try to **look** rich. They buy flashy things — houses, cars, jewelry — long before they've built any real financial foundation. Why? Because it feels good. The attention, the admiration, the dopamine boost — it gives them a temporary high.

But behind the scenes, the story is often very different.

To keep up appearances, they put themselves under constant pressure. They're stressed. Anxious. Many can't even sleep peacefully at night. They may appear successful on the outside, but inside, they're trapped in a cycle of debt, fear, and insecurity.

So now you must ask yourself:
Do you want to look rich — or do you want to be truly free?
Do you want to chase status? Or do you want to achieve **financial freedom** — and then, if you wish, become genuinely rich in the process?

Let's break it down.

What Is Financial Freedom?

Let me share **my own definition**.

I don't care how others define terms like financial freedom — because that's not why you bought this book. You could find those textbook definitions on the internet. But you're here to learn what life has taught **me** — through decades of hard work, trial and error, failure, success, and everything in between.

So here's what I've learned:

You are **financially free** when your income is consistently **more than your expenses**. But that's just the beginning.

You are **truly** financially free when you've built **passive income** — when your money works for you, even while you sleep. That's the next level. That's the freedom I'm talking about.

And that brings us to one of the most important concepts you'll ever learn:
The Two Types of Income — *Active* and *Passive*.

Active vs. Passive Income

Active income is the money you earn through your job or business — income that only flows when you're working. If you stop working, lose your job, or if your business slows down due to external issues like new competition, economic downturns, or unexpected events like pandemics, then your active income stops too.

That's why a **wise person plans ahead** — not just for the growth of their income, but for the day that income might slow down or disappear entirely.

Many people try to prepare for that by saving money. But relying on savings alone isn't a smart long-term solution. Why? Because savings eventually run out — especially when you can't replenish them. Worse, the value of your savings erodes over time due to **inflation**, meaning that the same amount of money buys you less and less.

So what's the better way?

The answer is **passive income** — money that flows in without your daily effort. It's income generated by your **money working for you**.

As I mentioned in Chapter One, once you earn active income, your next step is to **force your money to make more money**. That's the real breakthrough. Smart people build their financial future by:

1. Earning money actively
2. Saving and investing that money

3. Using it to generate **passive income** streams

Eventually, those passive income streams grow big enough not only to cover all your expenses — but also to generate surplus savings, which you can then reinvest to create even more streams.

That is true financial freedom.

Yes — you might already be earning enough active income to cover your lifestyle and put some money aside. That's great, and it *is* a form of financial freedom.
But it's not the **stable**, **reliable**, and **lasting** kind — because it depends on your continued work.

You're not here just to learn how to make money.
You're here to learn how to make **money that works for you** — even when you're not working.

That's the goal.

Your money can be the most **loyal, hardworking employee** you'll ever have.
It never complains.
It never betrays you.
It works 24 hours a day, 365 days a year.
So why wouldn't you make the most of that opportunity?

This is where I'm reminded of one of my favorite quotes — from someone I consider a legend and role model: **Warren Buffett**.

"If you don't find a way to make money while you sleep, you will work until you die."

Making lots of active income is wonderful — and I know that firsthand. When my online business took off (as you read in the previous chapter), I was making more money than I ever imagined. But I was still trading time for money.

Your mission isn't just to earn — it's to **earn**, then **invest**, then **multiply**.

That's what true wealth is built on.

So here's the path in simple terms:

1. Generate **active income** through business or your skills.
2. **Save** and manage that income wisely.
3. Use it to create **passive income** streams — your ultimate safety net and path to freedom.

Now, maybe you already have savings and don't need to start from zero like I did. That's fantastic — you're one big step ahead. But even so, I encourage you to read through the chapters where I explain how I built my **active income** from nothing. You'll discover strategies, insights, and ideas that can help you diversify, improve, and possibly even grow faster.

Once again, **don't skip any chapters**.
Even the ones you think don't apply to you may hold the idea that changes everything.

Who Is the Real Rich?

Most of the people who **look rich** are not truly rich. They may work hard and even earn a lot of money — but instead of using that money to build **passive income**, they spend it to maintain the illusion of wealth.

They invest in appearances: fancy houses, luxury cars, designer clothes, expensive jewelry — not assets that generate more income. And because their lifestyle depends entirely on **active income**, the moment that income stops, they're in trouble.

That's why, during the COVID-19 pandemic, you saw a sudden surge of luxury homes being listed for sale. Many of them were owned by people whose income vanished as soon as lockdowns began. These individuals didn't even have enough savings to cover their mortgage payments for a year or two — let alone maintain their entire lifestyle.

Now contrast that with someone who is **financially free**.

Yes, they may also look rich — but **not all who look rich are financially free**. And more importantly, **not all financially free people want to look rich**.

The truly rich are those who **own their time** — because their expenses are covered by **passive income**. They live in peace, not stress. Many of them live below their means, not out of necessity, but out of wisdom. Their financial foundation is built on security, not on showing off.

Over time, many financially free people do reach a point where they can afford luxurious homes and nice cars — but their lifestyle is supported by **income that doesn't stop**, regardless of the economy, competition, or external events.

That's the key difference.

People who only *look* rich live in fear — because their status can collapse at any moment.
People who *are* financially free live with peace — because they've built income streams that are **independent, stable, and lasting**.

So ask yourself:
Do you want to look rich?
Or do you want to live **free** — with peace of mind, regardless of what happens in the world?

This is a perfect time to bring in the example of one of the greatest investors in history — a man whose lifestyle and mindset embody this principle better than anyone else:

Warren Buffett has been a billionaire for decades and, at times, the richest man in the world. Yet he's never been interested in showing off his wealth.

He still lives in the modest house he bought in **1958** for **$31,500** in Omaha, Nebraska. He drives a simple car that's around ten years old. Despite owning a company that operates private jets, he rarely flies in one. He often eats low-cost meals like **McDonald's** — not out of necessity, but by choice.

His humble lifestyle reflects a deep truth:
Wealth doesn't need to be flaunted.
Living below your means is one of the key principles of long-term financial success.

Buffett once said:

"If you buy things you don't need, soon you will have to sell the things you do need."

That's wisdom worth remembering.

Please understand — I'm **not** saying that looking rich, living in a beautiful home, or driving a luxury car is bad.

It's not.

Those things are wonderful **when** you can truly afford them — when you're **financially free** and your **active and passive income** easily cover your lifestyle. When you're no longer worried about losing those things because you're not depending on unstable income to maintain them.

That's the key difference.

So yes — dream big. Live well. Enjoy the fruits of your success.

But do it at the right time — with the right foundation.

I hope you reach that point very soon. And you *will* — as long as you take the right steps, stay focused, and refuse to give up halfway.

Just remember:
This is a **long-term project**.
Financial freedom isn't built in a day.
It takes consistency, patience, and persistence.

But it's worth it — because the freedom it brings is priceless.

Should You Make a Lot of Money to Achieve Financial Freedom?

Making a lot of money — and managing it wisely — can certainly speed up your path to financial freedom. But that doesn't mean you **must** earn a lot to reach it. In fact, many people who earn high incomes **waste** their money and never become financially free. On the other hand, many people with modest incomes have **achieved it**, simply because they were disciplined, patient, and consistent.

Later in this book, I will share with you the impressive story of a cleaning lady who, despite her very low income, not only achieved financial freedom but eventually became a millionaire. I will also tell you about a janitor whose quiet consistency and discipline led him to the same result. These stories are powerful reminders that wealth is not reserved for those with high-paying jobs or prestigious careers. In fact, many people who earn large incomes remain trapped in debt and stress their entire lives, while ordinary workers with modest wages and extraordinary discipline end up building true wealth.

Financial freedom isn't about how much you make.
It's about how you think, how you act, and how consistent you're willing to be.

Bottom Line: Keep It Simple

Let's keep everything simple — because that's what I always aim for, in everything I do. When you want to do something well or solve a problem, the first and most important step is to **simplify** it.

So here's a simplified path to achieving **financial freedom** — and eventually, **wealth**:

1. Make Money Through Active Income

Start earning through an **active job or business**. In this book, I'll explain in detail how I made money online — step by step — so you can follow a similar path if you're just starting out.

If you're already making money through your own job or business, or you've built up savings, you're one step ahead.
Still, I recommend reading those chapters.
They'll give you valuable insights, fresh ideas, and strategies you may have never considered.

2. Save and Use Your Money to Generate Passive Income

Save a **reasonable portion** of your income until you can **put that money to work for you** — just like the cleaning lady I mentioned in the previous section.

In this book, I'll share multiple strategies that are even stronger and more scalable, to help you generate **passive income** and make your money **multiply itself**.

3. Repeat Until You're Free — Then Repeat to Build Wealth

Repeat the first two steps until your **passive income covers your lifestyle** and basic expenses. At that point, you've achieved **financial freedom**.

Then, keep going.
Repeat the cycle to build **wealth** — and to design the life you truly want to live.

In the next chapters, we'll focus on exactly how to do that — in real, practical steps.

Let's move forward.

Chapter 3
Make Money Online

Before we dive in, I want to say something important:
I hope you haven't skipped straight to this chapter just because the title sounds exciting.

If you did, I encourage you to go back and start from the beginning.

Why?
Because what I'm sharing here is not just another list of money-making tips and tricks. This isn't one of those recycled strategies you find in thousands of articles or videos — many of which are written by people who've never actually tried what they're promoting.

This book is different.

What you'll read here is based on **real experience** — what I've personally done, what has actually worked for me, and what I know **can work for you** if you stay committed.

And just as importantly, I'll also tell you **what doesn't work** — the strategies that are a waste of time, so you can avoid them and stay focused on what matters.

And... if you already have substantial savings or a steady active income from a job or business, you might be tempted to think this chapter isn't relevant to you — that you should skip ahead to the chapter about generating passive income. That would be a mistake too. Even if you're financially stable, this chapter will open your eyes to opportunities you may have never considered before. It can give you insights that could significantly enhance your financial journey. Skipping this chapter means missing out on valuable ideas that could complement and expand what you already have.

Financial Freedom Is the Ultimate Goal

Here, I must remind you once again that our ultimate goal is **financial freedom**. As I explained in the previous chapter, to achieve financial freedom, you must first **generate active income** through a job or business. Then, you must **make that active income work for you** by creating **passive income streams** — something I will explain in detail later in this book.

When it comes to generating active income, I can only share what I've done for myself — and that's **making money online through online business**. This path is far easier for most people because it can be started with a **very low budget — or almost no cost at all** — using the internet and working from home.

Of course, you might choose to generate active income through other kinds of businesses, which is perfectly fine. But you need to be fully aware of the **expenses, risks, and success rates** involved, which are **nowhere near as favorable as online business**.

Take a **brick-and-mortar business** like a coffee shop, for example:

To start, you'll need significant upfront capital for:

- Renting a location
- Buying equipment
- Decorating and setting up
- Advertising

And then you have to wait — often months — just to see if you'll even make a profit.

The hard truth?
Almost **80% of these kinds of businesses fail before their second year.**

So, choose carefully. **Be smart about the path you take to generate active income.**

Let's begin.

Different Groups of People When It Comes to Making Money Online

When it comes to making money online, there are **two main groups of people**.

The first group — which makes up the **majority** — are those who **don't have a product** to sell online.
I was part of this group when I started, and for people like us, there are plenty of effective options, which I will explain in detail.

The second group consists of people who **already have a product** that can be sold online. These individuals have an advantage: not only can they sell their own product online, but they can also earn money using the same methods available to the first group.

From now on, I will refer to these two groups frequently because every online money-making method applies to **one or both of them**.

The First Good News

Here's the best part:
When it comes to making money online, the sky is the limit.

Whether you have a product or not, you can still create a steady income online.

Starting with the Second Group: People Who Have a Product

Let's begin with those who already have a product. Many people believe that **any product** can be sold online — and while this is true to some extent, if your goal is to earn a **significant income and achieve financial freedom**, you need to understand **which products** have the potential to make a **fortune** online.

And remember, a product is not always what people imagine — a **physical, tangible item.**
Sometimes, **"you"** — your skills, your knowledge, your ideas — can be a product as well.

What's Next?

I'll start with an example to illustrate this idea, and then I'll dive deeper into both groups.

After that, I will **list all the ways you can make money online** — with the **pros and cons** of each — and show you:

- Which methods are best for beginners,
- Which are best for those with products,
- And how to choose the path that fits you best.

Don't worry — you won't get confused. I'll guide you step by step.

An Example to Learn From

Let me share an example that perfectly illustrates the kind of product that can bring true success online.

I know a Syrian gentleman who inherited a **family business of producing organic soap**, a craft passed down through generations. When the war in Syria began, he fled to Germany. Once there, he established a small workshop to continue producing organic soap — because it was the only skill he knew that could sustain him.

Today, he earns **between one to two million euros per year** in Germany. Not only is he financially free, but he is also rich.

Why?

The answer lies in the nature of his product. His soap is:

1. **Unique**
2. **High-quality**
3. **In high demand**
4. **Facing little or no competition**

These four characteristics are what make a product capable of building **serious wealth**.
If you have a product that meets these four criteria, you have a real shot at becoming a **multi-millionaire**.

The Reality Check

I share this example at the beginning of this chapter for a reason:
Many people believe their product is amazing and will make them rich — but the reality is often very different.

For example, I see many people trying to sell handcrafted items online, yet they generate **no sales at all**. Why? Because their products are not truly **unique or in demand** — and worse, there are **thousands (or even millions)** of similar products being sold online.

Some of these people spend **thousands of dollars** hiring web developers to build fancy websites, only to see zero sales. Why?

- Their products don't stand out.
- Their websites get **no traffic**.
- And even if they pay for advertising, the products are not attractive enough to make people spend money.

Think Twice Before Selling Online

If you have a product and believe it can sell online, **think twice** before investing your time and money. Ask yourself:

- Does my product have at least some of the four characteristics outlined above?
- Is it unique enough to stand out?
- Is there real demand for it?
- Can I compete effectively?

Many people spend large sums of money trying to sell products online — only to make **zero income**. Meanwhile, countless others, who have **no product at all**, make **substantial money online without spending anything**.

Be careful not to ruin your online business journey right at the start by making this mistake.

Now, if you don't have a product — or if your product doesn't have the qualities I explained earlier — but you still want to make money online, here's what usually happens:

Opportunists and scammers will tell you to "sell other people's products."
The first term you'll likely hear is **"dropshipping."**

This is the right time for me to clarify something important:
Yes, you **can** make money selling other people's products — I did it myself when I started, through **affiliate programs** (and I'll explain that in detail soon).

But I must warn you:
You won't make money through dropshipping.

I've seen countless people lose **thousands of dollars** to companies promising them a "fully automated dropshipping website." Platforms like Shopify are often involved, where they build a store for you and claim you'll "start earning as soon as your site goes live."

But here's the reality:

- **The more you wait, the less you earn.**
- These stores fail 99% of the time.

Why?
Because **thousands of people** already have the **exact same website** selling the **exact same products** — often at **lower prices** than yours.

Your website is new. It has **zero traffic** and **zero trust**. Even if you pour money into advertising, why would someone buy from you when they can get the same item from a well-known seller — possibly cheaper and faster?

Yes, you can make money selling other people's products — but **not through dropshipping**, and **not by paying thousands** for a cookie-cutter website with no uniqueness.

These "get-rich-quick" dropshipping schemes only make **the scammers rich**, not you.
They lure you in with promises of "thousands of products" on your site — but a website loaded with products **doesn't guarantee sales**.
Without a unique edge and traffic, it's just a digital store nobody visits.

Please be careful.
These scams are everywhere, and once you lose your money, **there's no way to get it back**.

Your desire to make money online should drive you to **real, proven strategies**, not traps designed to exploit your enthusiasm.

Whenever someone approaches you — whether online or offline — and promises to build a website or an online system (like a dropshipping store) that will supposedly make you **thousands of dollars every month**, and they ask you to **pay them a fee** to set it up, stop and ask yourself:

If what they're saying is true, why don't they set up the same system for themselves and make those thousands of dollars on their own?
Why are they trying so hard to convince you to pay them instead?

Isn't that a red flag?

Common sense says **it is**.

If they truly had a system that prints money, they wouldn't need you. They wouldn't be out there hunting for "clients" or "students" — because they'd already be busy making millions for themselves. The fact that they are selling you the "system" instead of using it should tell you everything you need to know.

I think I've warned you enough for now. If I remember anything else that you should watch out for, I will definitely tell you. Throughout this book, you'll notice that I frequently explain not only **what works**, but also **what is a waste of time and money** — because avoiding the wrong paths is just as important as choosing the right ones.

One of my main goals with this book is to **bring you closer to success** by showing you the most effective methods, while also helping you avoid the traps that could cost you years of effort, unnecessary frustration, and wasted money.

Now, let's **summarize the key ways to make money online**, whether you have a product or not.

Ways to Make Money Online

Before we dive deep, let's set the stage:

There are countless ways to make money online, but not all of them are worth your time. Some are outdated. Some are scams. And some are just distractions.

Here's what I'll do for you:
First, I'll give you a clear overview of the most common and proven ways to earn online — with a quick explanation of each.
Then, I'll **walk you step by step** through the **best, most profitable, and most reliable methods** — the ones with the **highest potential to create real income and long-term success**.

1. Starting a Website

When people think of making money online, starting a website is usually the first thing that comes to mind. Whether you have your own product or plan to earn by promoting other people's products or programs, **a professional, dynamic website remains the most powerful tool you can have** — and for good reason:

- It's one of the **most traditional and time-tested** paths.
- It's how I started my journey.
- And even today, despite all the new ways to earn online, **having your own website is still one of the most powerful and effective methods to build a sustainable income stream.**

But here's the truth:
We're living in a time where people are making **millions online without even having a website!** They use social media, online marketplaces, and other platforms that didn't exist (or weren't popular) when I started.

That's why, in this chapter, I'll not only teach you **how to build a profitable website** but also show you **other proven methods** that can bring results — even if you have zero technical skills or experience.

How It Was When I Started

Let me tell you — **building a website wasn't easy when I started out.**

Back then, if you wanted to have even a basic website, you needed to learn programming languages like **HTML**.
And if you dreamed of having a **professional website** with:

- Member areas
- Product listings
- Shopping carts
- Payment gateways
- Interactive tools

…you had to go even further — learning **ASP, PHP, and MySQL.**

I had no choice but to **learn all these skills myself.**
What began as a simple need turned me into a **full-fledged web developer and programmer.**

And that's not all.
As my online projects grew, I needed to understand:

- Dedicated servers
- Linux hosting
- Security and optimization

This learning curve was **tough, time-consuming, and expensive.**

The Trap of Hiring Developers

If you wanted to hire professionals to do this work for you, it often turned into a nightmare:

- You'd spend **a fortune** on developers.
- You'd get stuck in a **never-ending cycle** of paying for updates, fixes, and upgrades.
- And worst of all, many so-called "experts" were **either unskilled or downright dishonest,** milking clients for as much money as possible.

I've seen many people **give up their online dreams** after losing months — or even years — of time, money, and energy.

The Good News for You

Today, things are different.

You can create a **professional, modern, and fully functional website** without knowing a single line of code.
Powerful systems — which I'll reveal later — make it **easier, faster, and cheaper** than ever to launch your online business.

You don't have to be a programmer.
You don't need to hire one either.
You just need the right tools — and I'll show you exactly which ones work.

For now, consider this section as your **menu of options.**
I'm laying out all the **methods available** so you can choose the **one that excites you most** and gives you the **best chance to win.**

2. YouTubing

Everyone knows YouTube today — it's part of everyday life. But back in 2001, when I started my online business, **YouTube didn't even exist.**

Now, it has become **one of the biggest and most powerful online platforms in the world** — and I believe it is also **one of humanity's greatest inventions.**

In 2006, Google bought YouTube, and with Google's **technical expertise** and **financial backing,** it grew into the unstoppable giant we know today.

Here's the amazing part:
There are **thousands — maybe even millions — of people around the world who make a living solely through YouTube.**
Some of them earn **millions of dollars,** becoming incredibly wealthy — and many of them don't even own a website or know how to build one!

Why YouTube?

You can make **a lot of money** with YouTube — whether you have your own product or not.

- **If you have a product,** you can promote it on your own YouTube channel by creating engaging videos that highlight it.
- **If you don't have a product,** you can still earn by creating and uploading videos about a specific topic (your niche).

And here's the best part:
It costs **zero dollars** to become a YouTuber. It's completely free to start.

The Two Keys to Success on YouTube

However, success on YouTube doesn't come by luck. There are **two critical factors** that separate successful YouTubers from the rest:

a. Choosing the Right Niche

You **must** focus on a specific niche if you want to succeed.

- You cannot upload random videos about everything and expect to grow.
- YouTube's algorithm is highly intelligent and favors **consistent, focused content.**

Your goal is to find a **demanding niche** — one that has an audience but isn't overly saturated with competition. Then, create **high-quality videos** that solve problems, entertain, or inspire within that niche.

b. Video Creation and Consistency

You must develop at least a basic skill set in video creation and editing. Fortunately, many easy-to-use video editing tools are available today.

But above all, **consistency is king.**
Most successful YouTubers upload:

- **One video per day**, or
- **At least several videos per week**, depending on the niche.

Consistency builds trust with your audience — and it's exactly what the YouTube algorithm loves.

Is YouTube for Everyone?

YouTube is amazing. It is for everyone — and yet, it's not for everyone.
Why do I say this?

It's for everyone because I've seen countless people with **no technical or internet skills** make a lot of money on YouTube. For example, I've seen **blacksmiths, carpenters, painters, and many other skilled workers** simply record videos of their work in their workshops — using nothing more than a basic camera or even their smartphone — upload them consistently, and over time, their videos start getting views and generating income — sometimes **a lot of money** — despite their limited computer knowledge.

But at the same time, YouTube is **not for everyone.** I've also seen many people start a channel, even with valuable skills to share, but they fail to earn anything. The reality is that although many people make serious money on YouTube, **it doesn't guarantee success for everyone:**

- Many people start a channel, upload a few videos, and then quit.
- They get discouraged when they don't see immediate results — or they simply run out of ideas and motivation.

Don't worry — I'll explain **everything about YouTube in detail later,** so you can easily decide whether this is a path you want to pursue.

3. Becoming an Influencer

A famous YouTuber with a popular channel is, in many ways, also an influencer. However, the term **"influencer"** is generally associated with social media platforms like **Instagram** and **TikTok**.

You might ask: *Isn't YouTube considered social media too?*
The answer is **no** — not in the traditional sense. YouTube is primarily a **video search engine**, built to host, find, and recommend videos. While

it does have social features such as comments and community posts, its core purpose is not the same as Instagram or TikTok.

Influencers typically focus on platforms like Instagram and TikTok, where short-form, visually engaging content thrives. That said, many influencers also share their content on YouTube to reach a broader audience.

How Influencers Make Money

Once you build popularity on Instagram or TikTok, the opportunities to make money are virtually endless:

- You can promote your own products or services.
- You can collaborate with brands for sponsorships.
- You can earn through affiliate marketing and other creative partnerships.

At first glance, posting on Instagram or TikTok might seem easier than creating content for YouTube — and in many ways, it **is**.

However, when it comes to **long-term earning potential, YouTube still has the edge.**

- YouTube videos have a longer lifespan, continuing to generate views (and income) for months or even years.
- Monetizing YouTube videos is easier and more automated, and they tend to earn more because YouTube is backed by Google's powerful advertising network.
- Instagram and TikTok posts tend to have a much shorter "shelf life," requiring constant posting to stay relevant.

In short, while becoming an influencer on Instagram or TikTok can be lucrative, **YouTube offers higher potential and a greater chance of building a long-term income stream.**

4. Networking and Affiliate Marketing

Networking and affiliate marketing are among the most powerful ways to make money online — and some people earn a **substantial income** using these strategies.

In simple terms, networking and affiliate marketing involve **promoting other people's products or services** in exchange for a commission on each sale, sign-up, or action that comes through your referral. This can be done through:

- **Websites and blogs** (by writing content and adding affiliate links)
- **YouTube channels** (by reviewing or showcasing products in videos)
- **Social media pages** (by sharing links, running campaigns, or collaborating with brands)

Why Affiliate Marketing Works

Affiliate marketing is so popular because **you don't need your own product or service.**

- You can start with zero inventory and no upfront costs.
- You earn money simply by connecting the right product with the right audience.

Big companies like **Amazon, ClickBank, and ShareASale** have affiliate programs that allow anyone to promote products and earn a commission.

Networking as a Growth Engine

Networking is about **building connections and partnerships** — not just with companies but also with other creators, influencers, or business owners. By expanding your online presence and audience, you create opportunities to:

- **Refer new customers**
- **Recruit affiliates under you (in some programs)**
- **Leverage partnerships to increase visibility and sales**

The Risks and Scams to Avoid

While networking and affiliate marketing can be **highly profitable**, they also have **serious pitfalls.**

Many beginners fall into traps like:

- **Scam affiliate programs** that never pay commissions.
- **Ponzi schemes** that rely on recruiting members rather than selling real products.
- **Crypto rug-pulls** and other fraudulent schemes that promise big returns but steal your money.

These scams prey on people's desire for quick, easy money. **The truth is: real affiliate marketing requires effort, strategy, and trust.**

- You must only promote **legitimate products or services** that you believe in.
- You need to choose programs with a **solid reputation and proven payout history.**

What I'll Teach You

In the next sections of this book, I'll explain:

- **How affiliate marketing really works.**
- **The best and most reliable programs to start with.**
- **The strategies I used to turn affiliate marketing into a consistent income stream.**
- **How to spot scams and avoid losing time and money.**

Done the right way, **affiliate marketing can be one of the simplest and most scalable paths to financial freedom** — because your income grows with your audience, and eventually, your efforts can produce **passive income**.

5. Online Trading

Since we're talking about ways to make money online, **online trading is something I must include.** Why? Because I've been actively trading since around **2006–2007** — and it has been a significant part of my own journey.

I will cover online trading in **much greater detail** later in this book, but for now, I want to give you a clear understanding of what it really involves — and why it's very different from the other methods I've outlined so far.

The Truth About Trading

The first thing you must understand is this:

Online trading is risky.

- Unlike other online business models, trading involves putting your own money on the line.
- If you don't know what you're doing — or if you can't control your risks — you can lose everything.
- Many people have lost huge amounts of money in trading. Some have even **"lost their shirts"** and walked away broken.

This doesn't mean trading is impossible or bad — it just means you need to approach it with **serious caution, discipline, and education.**

The Learning Curve

Trading is not something you can learn overnight.

- It's not about memorizing a few strategies or watching a couple of YouTube videos.
- Becoming good at trading requires **time, patience, and constant practice.**
- It also requires developing the **right mindset** — because trading is as much about emotional control as it is about technical knowledge.

One of the biggest misconceptions is that you can become profitable just by taking a popular course or following some "guru."

The reality?

- Most of the so-called trading courses online are created by **digital marketers, not real traders.**
- They make money by **selling courses, not by trading.**
- As a result, their content rarely teaches what truly works in the markets.

Why Consistent Profitability Is Rare

To become what I call a **"consistently profitable trader,"** you need more than strategies — you need:

- **Deep understanding of the markets**
- **Solid risk management skills**
- **Years of practice**
- **Emotional discipline under pressure**

And here's the hard truth: **Very few people ever reach this level.**

Even professional traders — the real ones — **rarely share all their knowledge publicly.** Why would they? Most of them are too busy making money from trading itself.

Even if you do find a real trader who's willing to teach, **you still need to practice on your own — over and over — until your skills are sharp enough to generate consistent profits.**

Why I Still Believe in Trading

In spite of the challenges, **I believe online trading is one of the most rewarding skills you can ever learn.**

- If you learn it properly, it can give you **complete financial independence.**
- You can trade from anywhere in the world — with just a laptop and an internet connection.
- Unlike most businesses, you don't need employees, inventory, or customers.

But this freedom comes at a price: **discipline, patience, and years of practice.**

What I'll Teach You

In this book, I will:

- Share what I've learned over nearly two decades of trading.
- Explain **how I became profitable** — and what you must avoid.

- Show you **how to start trading safely, practice effectively, and build your skills** until you can trade with confidence.

If you're willing to be patient and treat trading as a **serious profession rather than a shortcut to quick riches,** it can change your life.

What Else?

There are indeed many other ways to make money online, but I won't focus on them in this book because **they aren't suitable for everyone.**

For example:

- **If you're a photographer,** you can sell your stock photos on platforms like **Shutterstock, iStock, or Adobe Stock.**
- **If you're a programmer, writer, or web developer,** you can work as a **freelancer** on platforms such as **Upwork, Fiverr, or Toptal.**

Many professionals make **serious income** through these specialized skills and platforms. However, as you can see, **these methods require a certain level of expertise or professional ability** (e.g., advanced photography or programming skills).

Since this book is designed to **work for everyone — regardless of background, experience, or profession** — I won't include these methods as part of the main strategies I teach here.

Now Let's Get Practical

We've covered the big picture — the different ways to make money online, who they're best suited for, and what to watch out for.

Now it's time to dive into the details.

Let's explore each of the **six main methods** to make money online in the **simplest, clearest way possible** — so that anyone who's serious about putting in the effort can follow along and take action.

Please remember: **you don't need to do all six.**
Choose **one or two** methods that suit you best. Start there. That's how you build your foundation.

Then, we'll move to the next stage — which I'll explain in the following chapter(s):
How to make your active income create passive income so that you can gradually move toward **financial freedom** — and eventually, if you stay the course, **real wealth.**

The Six Methods We'll Now Explore in Detail:

1. Starting a Website
2. YouTubing
3. Becoming an Influencer
4. Networking and Affiliate Marketing
5. Digital Photography
6. Online Trading

Let's begin.

1. Starting a Website

Websites are among the best and most powerful tools for starting an online business. However, they are not the only option, nor are they a requirement for making money online. For example, many YouTubers and network marketers don't have a website, yet they still earn a substantial income. That said, if you use a website properly, it can become a continuous and reliable source of income—no matter what.

Since launching a website was one of the very first steps I took when I began my online business journey, I feel it's important to start with it in this book. A website is what transforms you into a professional online businessperson, entrepreneur, and digital marketer.

Starting a Website: Step-by-Step Guide for Absolute Beginners

- What Is a Website and Why Do You Need One?

- What You Need to Start a Website
- Step 1: Choosing and Registering a Domain Name
- Step 2: Choosing a Hosting Provider
- Step 3: Installing WordPress (or Another Website Builder)
- Step 4: Designing Your Website
- Step 5: Installing Essential Plugins
- Step 6: Adding Content to Your Website
- Step 7: Securing and Maintaining Your Website
- Step 8: Launching Your Website

- What Is a Website and Why Do You Need One?

If you want to make money online, having a website is like having your own house or store on the Internet. It belongs to you. It carries your name, your message, and eventually, your income.

A website is simply a place on the Internet where people can visit, read what you have to say, learn from you, trust you, and eventually buy something from you — whether it's your own product or someone else's that you're promoting.

Think of it this way:
If YouTube, Instagram, or TikTok is like renting a small booth in a busy marketplace (where you're still at the mercy of the market owner), a **website is your own land and building**. No one can take it from you.

A website is truly **the strongest tool** you can have in your online business.

Even today, with so many other platforms available, **starting a website is still the most powerful and long-term way to build an online business.**
It gives you control, credibility, and the freedom to build something real — at your own pace, in your own way.

And don't worry if you think it's too technical.
I will guide you step by step. If you can follow a cooking recipe, you can start your own website. Even an 80-year-old grandma with no tech background can do this — and I'll prove it.

Let's begin with the very first thing you need:
your domain name — your website's name and address.

- What You Need to Start a Website

Before we start building your website, let's get familiar with the **three basic things** you'll need. These are simple and don't require any technical skills, but they're essential for creating a fully functioning website that belongs to you:

1. A Domain Name

This is your website's name and address on the Internet — like Google.com. It's what people type into their browser to visit your site. Your domain is your identity online, and once you register it, no one else can use it as long as you keep it renewed.

I'll soon show you how to choose a good domain and register it easily, step by step.

2. A Hosting Plan

Your hosting is where your website **lives online** — like renting space on the Internet to keep your website's files, pages, and content available 24/7.

Think of your domain name as your house's address, and hosting as the land the house sits on. Without hosting, your domain has nowhere to go. Don't worry — I'll show you how to get affordable and reliable hosting, even if you've never heard of this before.

3. A Website Builder (e.g. WordPress)

Once you have your domain and hosting, you need a tool to actually **build and manage your website**. That tool is called a website builder.

The one I recommend — and will teach you how to use — is called **WordPress**. It's free, easy to use, and powers over **40% of all websites** on the Internet, including big brands and small personal sites alike.

With WordPress, you can add pages, change your site's appearance, post articles, upload photos, and more — all without needing to write a single line of code.

These are the **only three things you need** to get started.

And the good news?
You can get all three — your domain, hosting, and WordPress — set up in less than an hour. And I'll walk you through every single step, just like a recipe.

Let's move on to **Choosing and Registering Your Domain Name** — one of the most exciting parts of creating your online business!

Step 1: Choosing and Registering a Domain Name

Your **domain name** is the first step toward building your presence online. It's what people will type in their browser to find you. Think of it like your business name, your brand, and your online identity — all in one.

Yours can be anything — it just needs to be:

- Easy to remember
- Simple to spell
- Related to your topic, product, or niche

How to Choose a Good Domain Name

Here are a few tips to help you pick the right one:

- **Keep it short and clear.** Avoid long or complicated words.
- **Use keywords if possible.** If your site is about fitness, try words like "fit," "strong," or "wellness."
- **Avoid hyphens and numbers.** These often confuse people and are hard to remember.
- **Stick with .com if possible.** It's still the most trusted and recognized extension.

- **Make it personal if needed.** Many great domain names are based on people's names — for example, MariaCooks.com or JohnWritesBooks.com.

And don't worry — your domain name doesn't need to be perfect. What matters most is that you **start** — and that you can remember and share your domain easily.

How and Where to Register Your Domain Name

Registering your domain name is very simple and takes just a few minutes.

There are many trustworthy domain registrars online, such as:

- Namecheap.com (offers domain + hosting together)
- GoDaddy.com (offers domain + hosting together)
- Google Domains
- Bluehost.com (offers domain + hosting together)

Here's what you'll do:

1. Visit one of the domain registration sites above.
2. Use their search bar to check if your desired domain is available.
3. If it's available, you can buy it immediately (usually costs around **$10 to $15 per year**).
4. Create an account and complete the payment.

That's it — you now own your website name!

Just make sure you **write down your account login info** somewhere safe, because you'll need it when connecting your domain to your hosting in the next step.

In the next part, I'll show you how to **choose your hosting plan**, and connect it to your new domain — so your website can come alive.

Step 2: Choosing a Hosting Provider

Now that you've chosen and registered your domain name, it's time to get a **hosting plan** — the space where your website will "live" on the Internet.

Let's keep it simple.
If your **domain name** is the address of your house, your **hosting** is the actual land and structure where everything is built and stored. Without hosting, your domain name leads nowhere.

What Is Hosting and Why Do You Need It?

A hosting provider gives you the space and tools to keep your website running. It stores your website files, keeps them safe, and makes your site available to the world 24/7.

Good hosting ensures that:

- Your website loads fast
- It stays online (no downtime)
- It's safe from hackers
- You can install WordPress and manage your site easily

Beginner-Friendly Hosting Providers

There are many hosting companies out there, but not all of them are beginner-friendly. Here are some of the most trusted ones that are perfect for those who are just starting out:

- **Bluehost** – One of the most popular for beginners. It offers free domain registration with hosting and has 1-click WordPress install.
- **SiteGround** – Known for excellent customer support and strong security.
- **Hostinger** – Affordable and simple, great for small websites.
- **Kinsta** – More advanced and powerful, but may be better for bigger.

If you're just starting, **Bluehost** is a safe and easy option. It's beginner-friendly and gives you everything you need in one place — domain, hosting, and WordPress setup.

How to Buy Hosting (Step by Step)

1. Go to the hosting provider's website (e.g. bluehost.com)
2. Choose a basic shared hosting plan (usually the cheapest is enough to start)
3. Register your domain (if you haven't already — Bluehost gives you one for free)
4. Create your account and make payment
5. Log in to your hosting dashboard (usually called cPanel)

That's it — your hosting is ready!

In the next part, we'll install **WordPress** — the free tool that allows you to build and manage your website with no coding or technical knowledge required.

Step 3: Installing WordPress (or Another Website Builder)

Now that you have your **domain** and **hosting** ready, it's time to bring your website to life by installing a website builder — the tool that lets you design and manage your site without any technical skills.

And when it comes to website builders, **WordPress is the best choice.**

Why WordPress?

WordPress is a free, easy-to-use platform that powers over **40% of all websites** on the Internet — from small personal blogs to major company websites.

Here's why I recommend WordPress, especially if you're just starting:

- It's **free** and open-source
- No coding knowledge required
- Thousands of **ready-made templates (themes)** to choose from

- Easily add features like contact forms, blogs, shops, or galleries
- Fully customizable as you grow

Simply put, **WordPress makes building a website possible for anyone** — even someone who has never touched a computer before.

How to Install WordPress in Just a Few Clicks

The good news is: most hosting providers offer **1-click WordPress installation.**
Here's how to do it:

Step-by-Step:

1. **Log in** to your hosting dashboard (you'll get this after buying hosting)
2. Look for an option that says **"Install WordPress"** (in Bluehost, this is under "My Sites" or "Website" section)
3. Choose your domain from the list
4. Click "Install"
5. Wait a few seconds while WordPress is installed
6. Once installed, you'll get a login link like: https://yourdomain.com/wp-admin
7. Log in using the username and password you created

That's it — you're now the proud owner of a real website powered by WordPress!

Alternative Website Builders (If You Don't Want WordPress)

Although I strongly recommend WordPress, some people prefer simpler tools like:

- **Wix** – Drag-and-drop builder, very visual
- **Squarespace** – Stylish templates, good for creatives
- **Weebly** – Very beginner-friendly and basic
- **Shopify** – Best if your focus is only selling physical products online

These are fine if you want something very simple or focused on visual design, but **WordPress gives you the most flexibility and growth potential**.

In the next part, I'll show you how to **choose a theme** and **design your website** so it looks beautiful and professional — even if you've never built a site before.

Step 4: Designing Your Website

Now that WordPress is installed, you're ready to design your website — this is where the fun begins!

Designing your site means choosing how it looks and how visitors interact with it. The good news is that WordPress makes this part easy with the help of **themes** and **plugins** — no design or programming knowledge required.

What Is a Theme?

A **theme** controls the appearance of your website — colors, layout, fonts, and overall style.

There are **thousands of free and paid WordPress themes** available. Whether you're building a blog, an online store, or a simple business site, there's a theme for you.

To keep it simple at the beginning, I recommend starting with a **free, lightweight theme** that looks clean and professional.

Here are some beginner-friendly options:

- **Astra** – fast, flexible, and great for almost any site
- **GeneratePress** – minimal, fast, and easy to use
- **OceanWP** – good for both blogs and businesses

These themes also come with **starter templates**, so you can import a complete website layout and just edit the content to make it yours.

How to Choose and Install a Theme

Here's how to pick and install a theme in WordPress:

1. Log in to your WordPress admin dashboard
2. Go to **Appearance → Themes**
3. Click **"Add New"**
4. Use the search bar to find a theme (like "Astra")
5. Click **"Install"** and then **"Activate"**

That's it — your new theme is live! You can now start customizing it.

Customizing Your Theme (No Coding Needed)

Once your theme is activated, you can customize it to match your brand or style.
Go to:
Appearance → Customize

There you can change:

- Your site's colors and fonts
- The homepage layout
- Your logo or site title
- Your menu and navigation bar
- Header and footer design

You'll see the changes happen in real time. And don't worry — **you can't break anything**. Just experiment and adjust until it feels right.

Set Up Basic Pages

To make your site functional and complete, you'll want to add a few essential pages:

- **Home** – The welcome page (we'll cover this in detail later)
- **About** – Tell your visitors who you are and what you do
- **Contact** – Let people get in touch with you
- **Blog** (optional) – Where you can post helpful content
- **Privacy Policy / Terms** – Required if you collect any visitor data

To create a page:

- Go to **Pages** → **Add New**, give your page a title, write your content, and click **Publish**

Now your site is starting to look like a real business — because it is!

In the next part, I'll show you how to **add functionality** to your site using **plugins** — tools that let you do almost anything you want, from collecting emails to setting up an online store.

Step 5: Installing Essential Plugins

Now that your website has a theme and a basic design, the next step is to give it **extra features** — things that your theme doesn't provide by default. This is where **plugins** come in.

What Is a Plugin?

A **plugin** is like an app for your website.
Just as you install apps on your phone to add new functions, you install plugins on your WordPress site to make it do more — without touching any code.

There are over **60,000 free plugins** available, plus many premium ones. You can find one for almost anything:

- Adding a contact form
- Speeding up your site
- Improving your SEO
- Backing up your website
- Creating an online store
- Connecting to email marketing tools

Installing a Plugin

Here's how to install one in WordPress:

1. Go to **Plugins** → **Add New** in your WordPress dashboard
2. Search for the plugin you want (e.g., "Contact Form 7")

3. Click **Install Now**
4. Once installed, click **Activate**

That's it — the plugin is live and ready to use.

Essential Plugins for Beginners

Here are some useful plugins to start with:

- **Yoast SEO** (or Rank Math) – Helps you optimize your site for search engines so more people can find you
- **Contact Form 7** – Lets visitors send you messages directly from your site
- **UpdraftPlus** – Creates backups so you can restore your site if something goes wrong
- **WP Super Cache** (or W3 Total Cache) – Speeds up your site for visitors
- **Wordfence Security** – Protects your site from hackers and threats

You don't need to install too many plugins — only what's necessary for your goals. Too many plugins can slow your site down.

In the next part, we'll move on to the fun and creative stage: **adding content to your website** — the heart of your online presence.

Step 6: Adding Content to Your Website

Your website is now set up with a domain, hosting, WordPress, a theme, and some useful plugins.
Now comes the part that will **bring it to life** — adding content.

Content is **everything your visitors see and interact with**: words, images, videos, and any information that helps them understand your message, product, or service.

Types of Content Your Website Needs

At the very least, every website should have:

1. **Home Page** – The first impression. This page should quickly tell visitors who you are, what you offer, and what action you want them to take.
2. **About Page** – Share your story, your mission, and why people should trust you.
3. **Contact Page** – Let visitors reach out easily through a form, email, or social media links.
4. **Blog or Articles Section** – Optional, but very effective for building trust, sharing expertise, and attracting search engine traffic.
5. **Products or Services Page** – If you're selling something, describe it here with clear benefits and pricing.

Creating a New Page in WordPress

Here's how to add a new page:

1. In your WordPress dashboard, go to **Pages → Add New**
2. Give your page a **title** (e.g., "About Me")
3. Add your **text, images, or videos**
4. Click **Publish**

That's it — your page is now live on your website.

Creating Blog Posts

If you plan to have a blog:

1. Go to **Posts → Add New**
2. Write your article title and content
3. Add relevant images
4. Choose a category (optional)
5. Click **Publish**

Blog posts are a great way to share helpful information and keep your site fresh — which search engines love.

Tips for Great Website Content

- **Write for your audience** – Focus on what they need and want to know
- **Keep it simple** – Avoid complicated words or technical jargon
- **Use headings, bullet points, and short paragraphs** – Makes content easier to read
- **Add visuals** – Images and videos make your site more engaging
- **Have a clear call to action** – Tell visitors exactly what to do next (sign up, contact you, buy, etc.)

Once you have your first pages and posts ready, your website will start feeling real — because it will be. From here, you can improve and expand over time.

Next, we'll move to **Securing and Maintaining Your Website** — so it stays safe, fast, and always online.

Step 7: Securing and Maintaining Your Website

Now that your website is up and running, you need to make sure it stays **safe, fast, and reliable** — just like you'd maintain a house or a car.

A neglected website can become slow, vulnerable to hackers, or even disappear entirely if something goes wrong. But don't worry — keeping your site in good shape is simple if you follow a few basic steps.

1. Keep WordPress, Themes, and Plugins Updated

WordPress, themes, and plugins release updates regularly to improve security, fix bugs, and add new features. If you ignore updates, you leave your site open to attacks.

To update:

- Go to your WordPress dashboard
- If you see an **Update** notification, click it and follow the instructions
- Update WordPress first, then themes, then plugins

2. Use Strong Passwords

Weak passwords are the easiest way for hackers to break in. Use a password that's:

- At least 12 characters long
- A mix of letters, numbers, and symbols
- Not related to your name, birthday, or anything easy to guess

You can use a password manager like **LastPass** or **Bitwarden** to remember them for you.

3. Install a Security Plugin

A security plugin will monitor your site for suspicious activity and protect it from common attacks.

Good options include:

- **Wordfence Security** (free and paid versions)
- **Sucuri Security**

4. Back Up Your Website Regularly

Backups are like insurance — if something goes wrong, you can restore your site to a previous working version.

You can automate backups with free plugins like:

- **UpdraftPlus**
- **BackWPup**

Set your site to back up at least once a week — more often if you post daily.

5. Use an SSL Certificate

An SSL certificate makes your website secure (you'll see a little padlock in the browser). Most hosting providers include this for free. It's essential for protecting data and building trust with visitors.

6. Monitor Your Website Speed

A slow site can make visitors leave before they even see your content. Use free tools like **Google PageSpeed Insights** to check your site's speed and follow their suggestions.

7. Remove Unused Plugins and Themes

If you're not using a plugin or theme, delete it. Unused items can become security risks and slow your site down.

With these steps, your website will remain safe, fast, and reliable — giving you the peace of mind to focus on growing your online business.

In the next and final part, we'll cover **Launching Your Website** — taking it live and sharing it with the world.

Step 8: Launching Your Website

You've set up your domain, hosting, WordPress, theme, plugins, and content. Your site is secure, and it's ready for visitors.
Now it's time for the exciting part — **launching your website** and showing it to the world.

1. Double-Check Everything

Before going live, make sure:

- All your main pages (Home, About, Contact, Products/Services) are complete and error-free
- Your navigation menu is easy to use
- Links work correctly and lead to the right pages
- Your site looks good on mobile and desktop
- Contact forms are working
- Spelling and grammar are correct

2. Announce Your Launch

Don't just quietly put your site online — tell people about it!
You can:

- Share it with friends and family via email or social media
- Post it on your Facebook, Instagram, or LinkedIn
- If you have a YouTube channel, make a short announcement video
- Join relevant forums or communities and share your site (without spamming)

3. Submit Your Website to Search Engines

Help people find you by telling Google your site exists.

- Go to **Google Search Console** (free)
- Add your website and submit your sitemap (your SEO plugin can generate this)

This step helps search engines index your pages faster.

4. Keep Posting and Improving

Launching your site is just the beginning. Success comes from **consistently adding content** and improving it over time.

- Publish blog posts regularly
- Update old content to keep it fresh
- Add new pages or features as your business grows

5. Be Patient and Persistent

Don't expect instant results. Websites often take months to gain steady traffic and income. But every article you post, every improvement you make, is building your online presence — and it all compounds over time.

Your Website Is Your Home Base

Now that you've launched, your website is your **home base** on the Internet. Whether you expand to YouTube, social media, or other platforms, your site will always be the place you control — the foundation of your online business.

Congratulations — you've just taken a major step toward building your online income and, ultimately, your financial freedom.

What to Do on Your Website

Now that your WordPress website is up and running, you might be asking:
"What exactly should I do with it?"

The truth is, with WordPress, you have **almost unlimited possibilities**. There's virtually nothing you might want to do that WordPress doesn't support — whether through its built-in features or the thousands of plugins available.

However, for most people starting out, the **core purpose** of a WordPress website — and one of the most powerful tools in digital marketing — is **blogging**.

Why Blogging Is So Powerful

Blogging is simply the act of publishing regular articles (called *posts*) on your website. But here's why it's so important:

- It drives **free, organic traffic** to your site — meaning people find you through search engines without you paying for ads.
- Organic traffic is **priceless** because once your content is online, it can bring you visitors (and income) for months or even years without ongoing costs.
- Paid advertising, on the other hand, can be expensive, complicated, and requires constant optimization to make a profit.

Blogging builds your **authority, trust, and visibility** — and trust is the foundation of all online income.

What Should You Blog About?

This is the golden question.

Technically, you *could* write about anything and everything… but that's a big mistake.

Search engines — especially Google — prefer sites that are focused on a **specific topic or industry**.

That's where the concept of a **niche** comes in.

Understanding Your Niche

A niche is a **specific topic or category** your website will focus on. Instead of being "about everything," you focus on one main subject and create most of your content around it.

Examples:

- Instead of "Fitness," focus on "Fitness for Busy Moms"
- Instead of "Cooking," focus on "Easy 15-Minute Healthy Recipes"
- Instead of "Travel," focus on "Budget Travel for College Students"

When you focus on a niche:

- Search engines start to see you as an **expert** in that area.
- Your audience knows exactly what to expect from your site.
- You attract the *right* visitors — people genuinely interested in your content or products.

How to Pick Your Niche

When choosing a niche, think about:

1. **Your Interests and Knowledge** – You'll be writing a lot about this topic, so pick something you enjoy and know about (or are excited to learn).
2. **Market Demand** – Make sure there are enough people searching for and interested in this topic.
3. **Competition Level** – Highly competitive niches can be harder to break into, but with the right approach, it's still possible.
4. **Monetization Potential** – Think about whether you can eventually sell products, services, or affiliate recommendations in this niche.

Blogging + Your Online Business

Once you've chosen your niche, your blog becomes the **engine** that brings people into your world.
From there, you can:

- Promote your own products or services
- Recommend other people's products for a commission (affiliate marketing)
- Build an email list for long-term customer relationships
- Increase brand awareness so people recognize and trust you

In the next section, we'll talk about **how to plan and create blog content** that gets noticed, attracts visitors, and builds your authority in your chosen niche.

How to Plan and Create Blog Content for Your Website

Once you've chosen your niche, it's time to fill your website with content that **attracts visitors, builds trust, and makes money**.
But here's the truth — the internet is full of noise. Millions of articles get published every day.
So if you want your blog to stand out, you need a plan.

Step 1: Understand Your Audience

Before you write a single word, ask yourself:

- **Who** am I writing for?
- **What problems** do they have?
- **What solutions** can I offer?

For example, if your niche is *Easy 15-Minute Healthy Recipes*, your audience might be:

- Busy parents
- College students
- Professionals who don't have time to cook

Knowing your audience helps you create content they actually care about.

Step 2: Do Keyword Research

Search engines like Google use keywords (the words and phrases people type into the search box) to match users with content.
If you want free, organic traffic, you must know what your audience is searching for.

How to find keywords:

- Use free tools like **Google Keyword Planner**, **Ubersuggest**, or **AnswerThePublic**
- Look for phrases that have a decent search volume but aren't overly competitive
- Make a list of ideas you can write about

Step 3: Create a Content Plan

A content plan is simply a list of blog post ideas organized by priority. Aim to create a mix of:

1. **Evergreen content** – Topics that stay relevant for years (e.g., "10 Quick Healthy Breakfast Ideas")
2. **Trending content** – Topics that are hot right now (e.g., "Healthy Meals for the Holidays")

Plan your posts for the next **1–3 months** so you always know what to work on next.

Step 4: Write Valuable, Helpful Content

When you write a blog post, focus on **helping your reader** first.

- Solve a problem
- Answer a question
- Teach something useful

Structure for an effective post:

1. **Catchy title** that makes people want to click
2. **Strong introduction** that explains what they'll learn
3. **Main content** broken into headings and bullet points for easy reading
4. **Conclusion + Call to Action** (tell them what to do next — sign up, share, buy, etc.)

Step 5: Use Images and Videos

Visual content makes your blog posts more engaging and easier to understand.

- Use free stock photo sites like **Pexels** or **Pixabay**
- Create simple graphics with **Canva**
- Embed videos if they add value

Step 6: Be Consistent

Consistency is key. Whether you post once a week or once a month, stick to your schedule.
Over time, your content library will grow — and so will your traffic.

Step 7: Promote Your Content

Publishing a blog post is only half the job — you need to **get it in front of people**.

- Share it on social media
- Send it to your email list
- Join relevant forums or communities and share when appropriate

Your blog is more than just articles — it's your **voice, your brand, and your connection to the world**.
When done right, each post becomes a little worker that brings in visitors, builds trust, and eventually turns strangers into customers.

Monetizing Your Blog

Creating valuable content is the foundation of your online presence — but to turn your blog into a source of income, you eventually need to **monetize** it.

However, **don't rush into monetization** when your site is brand new. In the early stages, your focus should be on:

- Publishing high-quality, niche-focused content
- Building trust with your audience
- Growing a loyal readership

During this time, collect your visitors' **email addresses** *(I will explain how)* and give them the chance to get to know you. Let them see that your site is genuinely useful, reliable, and worth returning to.

Once your website reaches a reasonable daily traffic level — for example, **1,000+ page views per day** — you'll be in a much stronger position to monetize it effectively.

How to Monetize Once You're Ready

1. Display Advertising

One of the most powerful methods is to **turn your website into an advertising network** for relevant brands and businesses in your niche.

Instead of relying on simple ad placement systems, you can use advanced tools like **Google Ad Manager**.

- This allows you to manage and control your own ad inventory
- You can sell ad space directly to companies or run programmatic ads from multiple sources
- You maintain full control over what appears on your site, ensuring that ads are relevant and brand-safe

This approach can generate far more revenue than basic ad services, especially once your traffic is steady and your audience is engaged.

Of course, advertising is only one way to monetize — there are several other proven strategies (below), so you can choose the ones that fit your niche, style, and goals.

2. Affiliate Marketing

This is one of the most popular and profitable ways to monetize a blog. You recommend products or services relevant to your niche, and when someone buys through your link, you earn a commission.

Example:

- If you run a cooking blog, you could promote kitchen tools from Amazon or online cooking courses from affiliate networks like ClickBank.

Steps to Start:

1. Join affiliate programs in your niche
2. Write helpful, honest reviews or tutorials
3. Place your affiliate links naturally in your content

3. Selling Your Own Products or Services

If you have your own products — digital or physical — your blog is the perfect place to sell them.

Examples:

- Digital products: eBooks, online courses, templates, printables
- Physical products: handmade crafts, merchandise, branded items
- Services: consulting, coaching, design work

This gives you the highest profit margins because you keep 100% of the sale.

4. Sponsored Content

Once your blog has a loyal audience, brands in your niche may pay you to write a post about their product or to feature it in your content.

- These can be one-time deals or long-term partnerships.
- Always disclose sponsorships to maintain transparency and trust with your readers.

5. Building and Selling an Email List

This is more of a long-term strategy, but it's one of the most powerful.

- Use your blog to offer a **free gift** (like an eBook or checklist) in exchange for visitors' email addresses.
- Once you have a list, you can promote your own products, affiliate offers, or even paid events directly to your subscribers.

Your email list is an **asset you own** — no algorithm or platform change can take it away from you.

6. Membership or Subscription Model

If you have highly valuable, niche-specific content, you can create a **members-only section** on your site.

- Members pay a monthly or yearly fee to access exclusive articles, videos, tools, or a community forum.

Important Reminder

You don't have to start with all these monetization methods at once. In fact, it's better to begin with **one or two**, master them, and then expand.
Too many monetization strategies at once can overwhelm you and distract you from creating great content.

A blog can be much more than just an online diary — it can become a **real business**, generating income month after month.
When you combine valuable content with smart monetization, your blog becomes a powerful engine for your financial freedom journey.

How to Build Your Mailing List

If you've spent any time learning about online business, you've probably heard the phrase:
"The money is in the list."

And it's true.
Your email list is **one of the most valuable assets** you can ever build online because it's yours. No algorithm change, no social media ban, and no platform shutdown can take it away from you.

When people join your mailing list, it means they've given you permission to contact them directly — in their personal inbox. That's powerful.

Why AWeber?

There are many email marketing platforms, but I recommend **AWeber** for beginners and professionals alike because:

- It's easy to use, even if you've never done email marketing before.
- It has strong automation tools to send emails automatically.
- It's reliable and trusted — it's been around since 1998.
- It integrates seamlessly with WordPress and most website builders.

Step 1: Sign Up for AWeber

1. Go to **AWeber.com**.
2. Choose the plan that fits your budget (they have a free plan to start).
3. Create your account and fill in the basic details about you and your website.

Step 2: Create Your First List

AWeber will guide you through setting up your first **email list** — basically, this is the database where all your subscribers' emails will be stored.

You'll name your list, add a short description, and set up your sender details (so your emails show as coming from you or your brand).

Step 3: Create a Sign-Up Form

Your mailing list needs a way for people to join it — that's where your **opt-in form** comes in.

- In AWeber, you can create beautiful sign-up forms without needing to code.
- Add fields like "First Name" and "Email Address" (keep it simple — the fewer fields, the better your sign-up rate).
- Once your form is ready, AWeber gives you a short code or HTML snippet to embed on your website.

You can place the form:

- In your blog sidebar
- At the end of each blog post
- As a pop-up when visitors arrive
- On a dedicated "Join Our Newsletter" page

Step 4: Offer Something Valuable

People don't give away their email addresses for nothing — you need to offer them a **reason**. This is often called a **lead magnet** or **freebie**.

Examples:

- A free eBook or guide
- A checklist or cheat sheet
- Access to an exclusive video
- A short email course

Make sure your freebie is directly related to your niche so the people joining are genuinely interested in what you do.

Step 5: Write Your First Follow-Up Email

Once someone subscribes, AWeber can send them an **automated welcome email** instantly.

- Thank them for joining.
- Give them the promised freebie.
- Tell them what they can expect from you in the future.

This first email sets the tone — so make it friendly, personal, and valuable.

Step 6: Stay Consistent

Your mailing list is like a garden — it needs regular attention.

- Send regular updates (once a week is a good start).
- Share new blog posts, tips, and exclusive content.
- Build trust before promoting anything.

When your subscribers know, like, and trust you, **monetization becomes natural** — and much more profitable.

A Great Example

Now is a good time to share a real-life example of a blog that generates a solid income — and in this case, it's not from someone running a huge corporation or a complex online empire.

Back in 2003, I learned the basics of blogging from one of the most well-known bloggers of that time, **Steve Pavlina**. He generously taught the steps of blogging for free on his own site, **StevePavlina.com**. I still remember one of his articles — over 7,000 words long — that explained *everything* we needed to know about starting and promoting a blog.

But Steve's blog is **not** the example I want to focus on here. Why? Because you might look at his professional-level success and think, *"I could never do that."*

Instead, I want to tell you about his wife's blog: **ErinPavlina.com**.

At the time, Steve created that blog for his wife, Erin, and it's still active today. Erin is a psychic. Whether or not you believe in her work is beside the point here. What matters is how she took a single skill, built a blog around it, and turned it into a consistent income stream — **without spending a fortune to get started**.

Since the very beginning, Erin has published an article in her niche every Wednesday, week after week, year after year. She sells reading packages directly through her blog, and judging by the loyal audience she's built, I'd say she's doing very well.

The lesson?
Your blog and the products or services you sell through it **don't need to be complicated**. You simply need:

- A clear niche
- Consistent content
- An offer your audience values

Do that well, and your blog could provide you with a comfortable living — or even a fortune.

Your Turn — Action Challenge

Take a few minutes right now to think about **your own skills, passions, or experiences** that others might find valuable. It doesn't need to be something extraordinary — it could be a hobby, a profession, a craft, or even life lessons you've learned.

Ask yourself:

- *What do I know that others might want to learn?*
- *What problem can I help people solve?*
- *What topic could I talk about every week without getting bored?*

Write down at least **three possible blog topics** that come to mind. This simple exercise could be the very first step toward building your own blog — one that could generate an income for years to come.

2. YouTubing

If starting a website is like owning a store on the Internet, then **starting a YouTube channel is like opening your own TV station** — one that can reach millions of people worldwide, 24/7, for free.

When I first began my online business back in 2001, YouTube didn't even exist. Today, it's one of the biggest platforms in the world — not just for entertainment, but for education, marketing, and business. In fact, for many people, YouTube *is* their full-time job, and some of them earn millions without ever owning a website or spending a fortune on advertising.

Why YouTube Works for Everyone

The beauty of YouTube is that **you don't need advanced technical skills** to get started. I've seen blacksmiths, carpenters, painters, gardeners, and bakers — people who barely know how to send an email — build successful channels by simply filming their work and posting it consistently.

All you need is:

- A camera (your smartphone will do just fine)
- A topic or skill to share
- The willingness to upload videos regularly

If you can point a camera, press "record," and talk about or show something you love, you're halfway there.

But… It's Not for Everyone

Now, I have to be honest. While YouTube can work for *anyone*, it's not the right path for *everyone*. I've also seen people start channels with enthusiasm, upload a handful of videos, and then quit because they lost motivation or didn't see instant results.

YouTube rewards **consistency, patience, and niche focus**. If you want to grow, you can't post about everything and expect success. You must **pick a niche** — a specific topic your channel will be about — and stick with it so the YouTube algorithm knows where to place your videos and who to show them to.

Choosing Your Niche

Your niche can be:

- **Educational** (teaching a skill, explaining concepts)
- **Entertainment-based** (comedy, music, storytelling)
- **Lifestyle-focused** (vlogging, fitness, cooking, travel)
- **Problem-solving** (DIY repairs, reviews, advice)

The key is to choose something that's:

1. **In demand** — people are already searching for it.
2. **Not too competitive** — so you have a chance to stand out.
3. **Something you can stick with** — because YouTube is a long-term game.

How YouTube Makes You Money

One of the reasons YouTube is so powerful is its **long content lifespan**. A video you upload today can still get views — and make money — months or even years later. Compare that to Instagram or TikTok, where a post often fades in relevance within hours or days.

When your channel meets the YouTube Partner Program requirements (currently 1,000 subscribers and 4,000 watch hours in the past year), you can start monetizing your videos. But that's just one method — as your audience grows, you can:

- Promote your own products or services
- Offer paid memberships for exclusive content
- Partner with brands for sponsorships
- Direct viewers to your website or mailing list

We'll go into detail later, but for now, remember: **consistency comes before monetization**. Build your audience first, then turn views into income.

Your YouTube Action Plan

If you want to try YouTubing, here's how to start:

1. **Create your channel** (it's free).
2. **Choose your niche** and stick with it.
3. **Plan your first 10 video ideas** — yes, 10! This ensures you won't run out of content in the first week.
4. **Record with what you have** — your phone is enough in the beginning.
5. **Post regularly** — ideally one video per week or more.
6. **Engage with your audience** — reply to comments, ask for feedback.

Beginner's Guide to Starting a YouTube Channel

Step 1: Understand What YouTube Is (and Isn't)

YouTube is not just a social media platform — it's a **video search engine**, owned by Google, with billions of users. This means your videos can be found by people all over the world — not just your friends and followers. Unlike Instagram or TikTok, where content quickly disappears, YouTube videos can continue attracting views for years.

Step 2: Decide Your Channel's Purpose

Before you even create your channel, be clear on **why** you're doing it. Is it to:

- Teach people something you know?
- Entertain and inspire?
- Promote your products or services?
- Build an audience for a future project?

The clearer your purpose, the easier it will be to plan and stick to your content.

Step 3: Choose Your Niche

Your niche is your **topic focus**. Don't try to cover everything — YouTube favors specialists, not generalists. Your niche should be:

- **Specific enough** to target a clear audience
- **Broad enough** to give you endless video ideas
- **Something you enjoy talking about** (or showing) regularly

Example niches:

- Gardening for small spaces
- Healthy cooking for busy professionals
- Simple DIY home repairs
- Storytelling for kids
- Beginner investing tips

Step 4: Create Your Channel

1. Go to YouTube.com and sign in with your Google account.
2. Click your profile picture (top right) → **Create a Channel**.
3. Enter your **Channel Name** (make it relevant to your niche).
4. Upload a **Profile Picture** (a clear photo or logo).
5. Add a **Channel Description** explaining what your channel is about and what viewers will get from it.

Step 5: Plan Your First Videos

You don't need expensive equipment or a complicated script to start.

- Write down **10 video ideas** related to your niche.
- Start with **short, simple videos** — 3–8 minutes is enough in the beginning.
- Your first videos can be basic — just aim to **add value** to the viewer.

Pro tip: Think about **searchable topics** people might look for on YouTube. If your niche is "indoor plants," titles like "5 Easy Indoor Plants for Beginners" will perform better than "My Plants."

Step 6: Gather Your Equipment

Start with what you have:

- **Camera**: Your smartphone is fine.
- **Microphone**: Good audio matters more than perfect video. If possible, get an affordable lapel mic.
- **Lighting**: Natural daylight works well, or use a basic ring light.

Step 7: Record Your First Video

- Find a quiet, well-lit spot.
- Speak clearly and naturally — pretend you're talking to one person.
- Don't aim for perfection. Your first videos are practice. You will improve over time.

Step 8: Edit Your Video

Editing makes your video smoother and more engaging. Free tools like **DaVinci Resolve** or **CapCut** are great for beginners.

- Cut out mistakes and long pauses.
- Add text overlays for key points.
- Include background music (only copyright-free music).

Step 9: Upload Your Video

1. On YouTube, click the **Create** button → **Upload Video**.
2. Add a **clear, keyword-rich title**.
3. Write a **helpful description** that tells viewers what the video is about.
4. Add **tags** (related keywords).
5. Choose an **attractive thumbnail** (custom thumbnails get more clicks).

Step 10: Stay Consistent

The key to YouTube success isn't one viral video — it's **consistent posting**.

- Aim for **1 video per week** (or more if possible).
- Keep improving your style and editing.
- Pay attention to what videos your audience enjoys most — and make more like them.

Step 11: Grow and Engage Your Audience

- Reply to every comment in the early stages.
- Ask viewers to **subscribe** and **hit the notification bell**.
- Share your videos on social media and your website (if you have one).

Step 12: Monetize (When the Time Is Right)

When you reach **1,000 subscribers and 4,000 watch hours** in the past 12 months, you can join the YouTube Partner Program to earn ad revenue. But don't rush — focus first on building an audience. Later, you can also earn from sponsorships, selling your own products, or driving viewers to your website.

Your First 90 Days on YouTube — Action Plan

The first three months are about **building momentum**, **finding your style**, and **getting comfortable on camera**. Don't obsess over views or subscribers yet — focus on creating, learning, and improving.

Days 1–7: Set the Foundation

- **Choose your niche** (pick one and commit for now — you can refine later).
- **Create your channel** with a clear name, profile picture, and description.
- Write down **at least 20 video ideas** in your niche so you'll never run out of topics.
- Gather your basic equipment (smartphone, microphone, lighting).

Weeks 2–4: Publish Your First 4 Videos

- Aim for **one video per week** to start.

- Keep videos short (3–8 minutes).
- Practice **clear audio** and good lighting.
- Don't stress about perfection — focus on finishing and uploading.
- Write keyword-rich **titles** and **descriptions** for each video.

Weeks 5–8: Refine and Learn

- Watch your **YouTube Analytics** to see which videos get more views and watch time.
- Experiment with **thumbnails** — try brighter images, close-ups, or bold text.
- Read and reply to every comment.
- Study successful channels in your niche to see what works.

Weeks 9–12: Build Consistency and Reach

- Keep posting at least **1 video per week** — or 2 if you can manage it.
- Share your videos on **social media**, in **relevant Facebook groups**, or on your **website/blog**.
- Begin creating a **call to action** in your videos: ask viewers to subscribe, like, or comment.
- Experiment with slightly longer videos (8–12 minutes) if your audience watches most of your current ones.

Your Goals by Day 90

By the end of your first 90 days, you should aim to have:

- **8–12 videos** uploaded
- A clear idea of **which topics perform best**
- A habit of **consistent posting**
- Your first **true fans** — people who watch most of your videos and comment regularly

Remember: The first 90 days aren't about going viral — they're about creating a habit, finding your voice, and laying the foundation for growth. The results will snowball if you stick with it.

3. Becoming an Influencer

You've probably heard the term **"influencer"** countless times, but what does it actually mean?

An influencer is simply **someone who has earned trust and attention in a specific niche** — so much so that their followers pay close attention to what they say, recommend, or endorse.

Yes, **popular YouTubers** are influencers, but the term is most often used for people who grow large, engaged followings on **social media platforms** like **Instagram**, **TikTok**, and **Facebook**.

Isn't YouTube a Social Media Platform Too?

Technically, no. YouTube is primarily a **search engine for videos** (owned by Google) with some social features. Social media platforms like Instagram and TikTok are designed for **quick, shareable content** — photos, short videos, and stories that keep people scrolling.

Why Become an Influencer?

Influencers can earn a living (and sometimes a fortune) without having a website or even selling their own products — simply by:

- Partnering with brands for **sponsored posts**
- Earning commissions through **affiliate marketing**
- Selling **their own products** or **services**
- Promoting **events, causes, or communities**

When you become known and trusted in your niche, **opportunities come to you**. Brands may reach out, followers may request your services, and your influence can grow beyond your chosen platform.

The Difference Between Instagram/TikTok and YouTube

Many beginners assume social media is *easier* than YouTube — and in some ways, it is. But there are trade-offs:

Instagram & TikTok

- Faster growth is possible
- Easier to create quick content
- Great for trends and visual appeal
- **Short shelf life** — your post may be forgotten in hours or days
- Requires **constant posting** to stay relevant

YouTube

- Slower initial growth
- More work to create videos
- **Much longer shelf life** — a good video can get views for *years*
- Monetization is more **automatic and scalable** through Google-backed systems

For long-term income and evergreen content, **YouTube often wins**. But for fast attention and personal connection, **Instagram and TikTok shine**.

How to Start as an Influencer (Even from Zero)

Step 1 — Choose Your Platform
Pick one platform to start with — don't try to master them all at once. If you love short videos, TikTok may be your best choice. If you prefer photos and lifestyle posts, Instagram might be better.

Step 2 — Define Your Niche
Just like with blogging or YouTube, **focus** is everything. People follow influencers because they know what to expect from them.

Step 3 — Create Quality Content Consistently
Post regularly. For Instagram, that might mean 3–5 posts per week plus Stories. For TikTok, it could be daily short videos.

Step 4 — Engage With Your Audience
Reply to comments, answer DMs, and be genuinely interested in your followers. Influence is built through relationships, not just numbers.

Step 5 — Collaborate
Work with other creators to cross-promote and reach new audiences.

Step 6 — Monetize
Once you have a consistent following, you can partner with brands, promote affiliate products, or launch your own offers.

Final Tip: The fastest way to grow as an influencer is to **give value first** — inspire, teach, entertain, or inform — without asking for anything in return. The trust you build will become the foundation of your income.

4. Networking and Affiliate Marketing

When people hear the term **"networking"** in an online business context, they often think of meeting others, building relationships, and finding ways to collaborate. And that's exactly what it is — **creating connections that lead to opportunities**.

When combined with **affiliate marketing**, networking becomes a powerful way to earn money online by promoting other people's products or services and earning a commission for every sale or referral you make.

Affiliate Marketing in Simple Terms

Affiliate marketing is like being a commission-based salesperson — **but online**.

Here's how it works:

1. You find a product, service, or program you believe in.
2. You sign up for its **affiliate program** (many are free to join).
3. You get a unique **tracking link**.
4. You promote that link through your **website, blog, YouTube channel, social media, or email list**.
5. When someone clicks and buys, you earn a commission.

Affiliate marketing is extremely popular because:

- You don't have to create your own product.
- You can promote products that already sell well.
- You can earn **passive income** from content that works for you 24/7.

Networking in the Online Space

In the digital world, networking often means:

- Building **relationships with other entrepreneurs** in your niche.
- **Collaborating** on joint projects or content.
- **Exchanging referrals**.
- Helping each other grow audiences.

Done right, networking can multiply your reach and income.

The Dark Side of "Networking"

Unfortunately, the term "networking" is sometimes misused — especially in the world of **MLM (Multi-Level Marketing)**, **pyramid schemes**, and **Ponzi schemes**.

- **MLM / Pyramid Schemes:** These focus more on **recruiting people** than selling real products. You earn money mainly from bringing in new members, who also have to recruit to earn.
- **Ponzi Schemes:** These use money from new investors to pay earlier investors, instead of using real profits. They **always collapse**, leaving most people with heavy losses.

The danger is that you can get involved in such schemes **without realizing it**. Sometimes they are disguised as legitimate business opportunities, and by the time you understand what's happening, you could be breaking the law or facing financial loss.

How to protect yourself:

- Research the company thoroughly.
- Avoid any business where the main income comes from recruiting, not real product sales.
- Stay away from "too good to be true" promises.

- If there's no clear, valuable product or service, walk away.

Legitimate Networking & Affiliate Marketing

When done ethically, affiliate marketing and networking can be one of the safest, most reliable ways to make money online. For example:

- Promoting **software tools** you use and trust.
- Recommending **books, courses, or equipment** relevant to your niche.
- Partnering with other businesses to run **joint promotions**.

You build relationships, create value, and earn commissions **without ever misleading your audience**.

Combining Your Website, YouTube Channel, and Social Media for Networking & Affiliate Marketing Success

If you already have — or plan to build — **a strong website, a YouTube channel, and active social media accounts**, you hold **the three most powerful tools in the online marketing world**. Each one is strong on its own, but when you combine them strategically, their impact multiplies.

Think of it like this:

- Your **website** is your **home base**.
- Your **YouTube channel** is your **broadcast station**.
- Your **social media** is your **conversation hub**.

Used together, they create a powerful "web" of influence that makes Networking & Affiliate Marketing far more effective.

1. Using Your Website as the Hub

Your website is where all your traffic should **eventually land** — whether it comes from YouTube, Instagram, TikTok, Facebook, or anywhere else.

On your site, you can:

- Publish **detailed articles** that explain and promote affiliate products.
- Create **landing pages** for special offers.
- Capture **email addresses** to build your mailing list (crucial for long-term income).
- Build **trust** by sharing stories, tutorials, and reviews.

Example: You make a YouTube video reviewing a microphone you use. In the description, you link to your website, where viewers can read a detailed review with your affiliate link.

2. YouTube: The Traffic Magnet

YouTube is perfect for **demonstrating** affiliate products, sharing tutorials, and showing results in action.

Ways to integrate it with networking & affiliate marketing:

- **Product Reviews & Unboxings:** Showcase a product and link viewers to your website for more details.
- **Tutorials & How-To Videos:** Teach something valuable, and naturally mention tools you use — with your affiliate links on your site.
- **Behind-the-Scenes Content:** Let viewers see how you use certain products or services in real life.

YouTube also makes you **more relatable**. When people see and hear you regularly, they feel like they know you — which builds trust, the most important currency in affiliate marketing.

3. Social Media: The Relationship Builder

Platforms like Instagram, TikTok, Facebook, and LinkedIn help you:

- **Stay visible** daily without having to publish long content.
- Share **quick tips, updates, and special offers**.
- Drive traffic to both your YouTube channel and your website.

Networking also thrives on social media because it's easy to **connect with influencers, potential partners, and other creators**. A single collaboration can bring thousands of new eyes to your affiliate offers.

4. The Power of the "Triangle" Strategy

When you combine all three platforms effectively, you create a **self-feeding cycle**:

1. **YouTube Video → Website:** A tutorial on YouTube links viewers to your website for a free guide or a full review.
2. **Website → Social Media:** Your website encourages readers to follow you on Instagram or TikTok for quick daily tips.
3. **Social Media → YouTube & Website:** Social media posts link back to your videos or articles, bringing more traffic and trust.

Every platform supports the others — **and the more touchpoints you have with people, the more likely they are to buy through your affiliate links**.

5. Why This Works So Well for Networking

Networking is about **visibility and trust**. If people see you everywhere — on your site, YouTube, and social platforms — they naturally view you as **an authority in your niche**.

This means:

- More partnership offers from other creators.
- More invitations to promote high-paying affiliate programs.
- More loyal followers who actually listen to your recommendations.

When someone sees your advice in a blog post, a YouTube video, and a TikTok clip — **all saying the same thing, all leading back to your affiliate link** — the trust and familiarity multiply, and so do your earnings.

5. Digital Photography

Digital photography is one of my absolute favorite methods for making money online. The strange part, however, is that although I love it so much, I have personally never made any money from it—simply because I never dedicated serious time to it. I became busy with other endeavors I pursued, and photography remained more of a passion than a business for me.

The good news for you is that digital photography can indeed be a profitable online venture—especially if you already have a strong passion for it. Unlike many other online income methods, this one is deeply rooted in creativity and self-expression. It's less about business in the beginning and more about art. That's why, to succeed in this field, you must truly love photography. Passion is the fuel that keeps you learning, experimenting, and improving, and it's also what makes your work stand out in a competitive market.

My journey into digital photography began when I bought a Sony 8-megapixel digital camera with the first money I earned online. At the time (over 21 years ago), it was an exceptional camera, and even now it still holds up well. It had a Carl Zeiss lens, which gave my photos outstanding clarity and quality. I started taking pictures purely out of passion and creativity, without ever taking a course or formal training.

When I moved to Canada, I decided to take it a step further. I signed up for an account with **iStockphoto.com**, a platform where photographers can sell their photos online. During that time, I discovered that some photographers were earning as much as **$16 million per year** through stock photography. That blew my mind, and I was eager to follow in their footsteps.

So, I rushed to sign up. But I never uploaded my photos, because, as I mentioned earlier, I became too busy with other areas of my business and life.

In spite of this, some people actually wanted to buy my photos because I used to share them on the photo gallery of one of my websites at that time. However, I never pursued it seriously and therefore never sold any of my photos.

However, **you can absolutely do this.** If you have a passion for photography and are willing to put in the time, you can get accepted, start building your portfolio, and eventually generate a real income stream. And I'll explain exactly how you can start:

1. Getting Started: Gear + Mindset

You don't need the most expensive camera. Even a mid-range DSLR, mirrorless, or high-quality smartphone works—**as long as the photos meet iStock's technical standards**: sharp, clean, and free from noise or logos. Good lighting and composition matter more than expensive gear.

2. Learning the Basics

Before applying to iStock, learn the fundamentals of exposure, lighting, and editing. Free YouTube courses or short, affordable photography classes are enough. Remember: iStock reviewers look for **technical quality first.**

3. Creating an iStock Contributor Account

Go to **iStockphoto.com** and look for the **"Sell Stock" or "Become a Contributor"** link.

- You'll be redirected to **Getty Images/iStock Contributor**.
- You'll provide ID verification, tax information, and payment details.
- Once registered, you'll need to **submit sample images** for review.

4. Passing the Test — The 3 Sample Photos

This is the **first hurdle**. iStock asks you to upload three of your best photos:

- **People**: lifestyle or portrait with a signed **model release**.
- **Object/Product**: something clean, well-lit, with no logos.
- **Concept/Lifestyle**: a usable stock image with space for text.

✓ If approved, you'll get access to upload more.
✗ If rejected, they'll tell you why (noise, logos, exposure, etc.). You can reapply later.

5. Uploading and Managing Your Portfolio

Once approved:

1. Log in to the **iStock Contributor portal**.
2. Upload your images (JPG, high resolution, sRGB color space).
3. Add **titles, descriptions, and keywords**—this is crucial because buyers search using keywords.
4. Submit them for review. Each file gets checked by iStock inspectors.
5. Approved files become live in the iStock marketplace and on Getty Images.

6. What Sells Best on iStock

iStock buyers are usually **businesses, marketers, bloggers, and designers**. They want:

- **Real-life lifestyle shots**: working from home, fitness, family, health.
- **Business/technology**: laptops, fintech, AI, meetings.
- **Seasonal content**: holidays, school, tax season.
- **Objects on plain backgrounds**: products, tools, food.

Tip: Think like a **graphic designer**—leave **copy space** in your photos so buyers can add text or logos.

7. Scaling Up

iStock rewards **consistency and volume**. Don't just upload a handful of photos and stop. Aim to build a **portfolio of hundreds, then thousands** over time. The bigger your portfolio, the more chances buyers have to find your work.

8. Royalties & Payments

- On iStock, you typically earn **15%–45% commission** depending on exclusivity and sales volume.
- Payments are sent monthly (PayPal, Payoneer, or Skrill) once you reach the minimum payout threshold.
- One image can sell **hundreds of times over years**, creating **passive income**.

9. Rinse & Repeat

The system is simple:
Shoot → Edit → Upload → Keyword → Submit → Sell → Repeat.
Your first sale might take time, but once it happens, you'll see how addictive it can be. Each photo is like planting a small seed that can keep paying you for years.

Mini-Guide: Passing the iStock "Three Approval Images" Test

Before you can start selling on iStockphoto, you need to pass the **entry test**: submitting **three sample images** that meet their technical and creative standards. Many beginners fail here—not because they lack talent, but because they don't know what iStock reviewers look for. Let's make sure you pass on the first attempt.

1. Understand What iStock Wants

- **Commercial Quality**: Photos must be sharp, well-lit, and free from dust, noise, and logos.
- **Useful for Buyers**: Images should be versatile—designers need photos they can use in ads, blogs, websites, or presentations.
- **No Legal Issues**: No copyrighted material, visible logos, or recognizable people without a signed model release.

2. Choose the Right Subjects for Your Three Photos

Here's a winning formula that works for many beginners:

1. **Lifestyle / People Shot**
   - Example: A person working on a laptop at home, a family enjoying dinner, or someone jogging in the park.
   - Make sure faces are clear, lighting is natural, and you have a signed **model release**.
2. **Object / Product Shot**
   - Example: A cup of coffee on a clean table, a smartphone on a desk, or fresh fruit on a kitchen counter.
   - Use a plain background with good lighting so the object "pops."
3. **Concept / Creative Shot**
   - Example: A road leading to the horizon (symbolizing "journey"), hands exchanging money (symbolizing "business"), or a lightbulb glowing (symbolizing "ideas").
   - These sell well because they carry universal meanings.

3. Technical Checklist Before Submission

Run each photo through this quick QA list:

- High resolution (at least 1600px on the longest side; ideally much larger).
- JPG format, sRGB color profile.
- No visible noise, blur, or dust.
- No logos, watermarks, or trademarks.
- Good composition (rule of thirds, clean subject, balanced framing).
- Natural lighting or soft artificial lighting (avoid harsh shadows).

4. Editing & Polishing

- Use **Lightroom, Photoshop, or free alternatives** like GIMP to adjust brightness, contrast, and sharpness.
- Don't overdo filters—iStock buyers want clean, natural images they can adapt.
- Zoom in at 100% to check for imperfections (noise, dust spots).

5. Submitting Your Photos

- Log in to your iStock contributor account.
- Upload your three best shots.
- Add short titles and keywords (keep it simple at this stage).
- Submit for review and wait for the decision.

6. If You Get Rejected

Don't worry—it happens to many first-timers. If rejected:

- Review the reasons iStock gives (too dark, too noisy, subject not commercial).
- Correct those issues and try again after the waiting period.
- Remember, one rejection doesn't mean you're not good enough—it just means your photos need tweaking.

✅ **Pro Tip:** Look at the best-selling photos on iStock to understand what passes. Notice the lighting, subjects, and clean style. Then try to match that standard with your own touch.

Three Ready-Made Photo Project Ideas

(For iStock's 3-Photo Approval Test)

These are **step-by-step mini-shoots** designed to check all the boxes that iStock reviewers look for: clean, commercial, and versatile images.

1. Lifestyle Shot – "Work From Home"

Objective: Capture a relatable, everyday moment that buyers can use in blogs, ads, or presentations.

What You Need:

- A desk or table
- Laptop (or tablet)
- Coffee cup or notebook
- A friend/family member (or yourself, using timer mode)

Steps:

1. Set up a clean, uncluttered desk near a window for natural light.
2. Place laptop + cup + notebook neatly (symmetry helps).
3. Have the subject sit casually, typing or sipping coffee.
4. Take multiple angles: straight-on, from above (flat-lay style), and from the side.
5. Ensure the face is either smiling naturally or not visible (both work commercially).

Checklist:

- Clear, sharp focus on the person and objects.
- No brand logos (cover them with tape or use generic items).
- Natural, bright lighting.

2. Object Shot – "Coffee & Inspiration"

Objective: Create a clean product-style shot that can symbolize productivity, mornings, or lifestyle.

What You Need:

- A plain white or light-colored background (poster board works great).
- A coffee cup, pen, and small notebook.
- A well-lit area near a window.

Steps:

1. Place the poster board on a flat surface (or tape it to a wall for a seamless backdrop).
2. Arrange the coffee cup, notebook, and pen neatly.
3. Shoot from above (flat-lay) and at a 45° angle.
4. Make sure the background looks clean and minimalistic.
5. Take several shots, adjusting the angle slightly each time.

Checklist:

- Crisp focus, no shadows falling across the cup.
- White balance set so whites look pure (not yellow/blue).

- Minimal editing needed—buyers love clean shots.

3. Conceptual Shot – "Journey Ahead"

Objective: Symbolize progress, adventure, or opportunity—concept shots sell very well.

What You Need:

- An outdoor location (quiet road, pathway, or trail).
- Good natural light (early morning or late afternoon is best).

Steps:

1. Find a straight path/road with perspective lines leading into the horizon.
2. Stand low (crouch or kneel) so the road/path takes up most of the frame.
3. Frame so the horizon is at the top third of the photo (rule of thirds).
4. Take multiple shots with slight variations in angle.
5. Optional: include a silhouette of a person walking away (adds "journey" meaning).

Checklist:

- No cars, signs, or identifiable people in the background.
- Sharp focus from foreground to background.
- Balanced, bright lighting.

✓ **Pro Tip:** After taking these three projects, review them in editing software at 100% zoom to check for dust, blur, or noise. Clean them up before submitting.

Step-by-Step Guide: Submitting Your First Photos on iStockphoto

Step 1: Create Your Contributor Account

1. Go to iStockphoto Contributor Page (this redirects to Getty Images Contributor).
2. Click **"Apply"** or **"Join Now."**
3. Sign up with an email address and create a **Getty Images Contributor account** (iStock uses the same system).
4. Verify your email by clicking the confirmation link they send.

✅ **Tip:** Use a professional-sounding username (buyers and reviewers see it). Avoid nicknames.

Step 2: Set Up Your Profile

1. Log in to your contributor dashboard.
2. Add a **profile photo** (optional but professional).
3. Write a short **bio** – something like *"Passionate digital photographer specializing in lifestyle, nature, and conceptual imagery."*
4. Add **payment details** (PayPal is the easiest method worldwide).

Step 3: Prepare Your Three Approval Photos

- Pick your **best 3 images** (use the project ideas we created earlier).
- Check them carefully:
    - Minimum 4 megapixels (ideally 12MP+).
    - No watermarks, no logos.
    - Sharp, clean, noise-free.
    - Edited lightly (fix brightness, contrast, white balance, crop).

Step 4: Upload the Three Images for Review

1. In your contributor dashboard, click **"Upload & Submit Content."**
2. Drag and drop your 3 photos into the uploader.
3. Fill out the details:
    - **Title:** Keep it short and descriptive (e.g., "Man working on laptop at home").

- - **Description:** 1–2 sentences explaining the photo's content and context.
  - **Keywords:** Add 10–20 relevant words buyers might search (e.g., "remote work, home office, laptop, freelance, digital nomad").
  - **Category:** Choose the closest match (e.g., Lifestyle, Nature, Conceptual).
4. Mark if it has **recognizable people or property**:
   - If yes, you need a **model release** (signed form by the person).
   - If no, select "No."

✅ **Pro Tip:** For your first 3 photos, avoid people/logos/brands so you don't need model or property releases yet.

Step 5: Submit for Review

1. After entering all details, click **"Submit for Review."**
2. Wait 3–5 business days (sometimes faster).
3. Check your email – they'll tell you if you're approved.

Step 6: After Approval – Start Uploading More Photos

1. Once approved, you can upload **unlimited photos** (though each is reviewed before going live).
2. Stick to a **niche** (e.g., lifestyle, food, landscapes).
3. Upload consistently – weekly uploads improve visibility.
4. Track your sales in the dashboard (earnings are reported monthly).

Step 7: Cashing Out

- Once your earnings reach the minimum payout threshold ($100 for PayPal), you can request payment.
- Payments are sent monthly, usually around the 20th.

Remember, your first 3 photos are just the beginning. Passing the approval gate is like unlocking the door to a global marketplace. From there, it's a game of **consistency**: shoot, upload, sell, repeat. Just like trading or any other online income stream, success in stock photography is about patience, persistence, and steady growth.

Common Rejection Reasons + Quick Fixes (iStock / Getty Images Contributor)

1. Technical Quality Issues

- **Reason:** Photos are too noisy, blurry, overexposed/underexposed, or lack sharpness.
- **Fix:**
    - Always shoot in good light (avoid dim rooms).
    - Use a tripod to avoid camera shake.
    - Edit lightly in Lightroom/Photoshop: adjust exposure, contrast, and sharpness.
    - Export at high resolution with minimal compression.

2. Composition Problems

- **Reason:** The subject is poorly framed, cluttered, or doesn't look professional.
- **Fix:**
    - Follow the **rule of thirds**.
    - Keep backgrounds clean and simple.
    - Remove distracting objects before shooting.
    - If shooting products/objects, use a plain backdrop (like white or black).

3. Intellectual Property Issues

- **Reason:** Logos, brand names, or copyrighted items appear (even accidentally).
- **Fix:**
    - Avoid including brands (Apple logo, Nike shoes, Coke bottle).
    - Blur or crop out logos.
    - Choose neutral objects or generic props instead.

4. Model or Property Release Missing

- **Reason:** A recognizable person (or private property/artwork) is in the photo without a signed release.
- **Fix:**
    o For your first 3 photos, avoid people or private spaces completely.
    o Use nature, landscapes, food, or objects.
    o If you want to use people later, download iStock's **model release form**, have them sign, and upload it.

5. Oversaturation or Over-Editing

- **Reason:** Colors look too unnatural, filters are too heavy, or editing is obvious.
- **Fix:**
    o Keep editing natural.
    o Adjust exposure/contrast gently.
    o Avoid Instagram-style filters.

6. Irrelevant or Poor Keywords

- **Reason:** Keywords don't match the photo, or too few/too many are added.
- **Fix:**
    o Add 10–20 relevant keywords.
    o Think like a buyer: "What would someone type to find this photo?"
    o Example: A cup of coffee on a desk → keywords: coffee, desk, workspace, morning, caffeine, productivity, home office.

7. Not Meeting Minimum Requirements

- **Reason:** Photo resolution is too small, wrong file format, or not JPG.
- **Fix:**
    o Ensure images are **JPG**, at least **4MP resolution**.
    o Save at the **highest quality** setting (quality 12 in Photoshop, 100% in Lightroom).

Quick Encouragement

- **Rejection is normal.** Even pros get rejected sometimes.
- Use rejections as **feedback** — iStock usually gives a short reason (e.g., "focus issue" or "intellectual property").
- Adjust, re-shoot, re-edit, and resubmit.
- Each rejection is one step closer to learning what stock agencies want.

Fast-Track Approval Checklist (10 Points Before Submitting to iStock)

1. **Resolution Check** → Minimum 4MP, ideally much higher (e.g., 4000px on the long side).
2. **File Format** → Export as **high-quality JPG**, sRGB color space.
3. **Sharpness & Focus** → Zoom to 100% — is the subject sharp and clear?
4. **Lighting** → Well lit, no harsh shadows, no blown-out highlights.
5. **Clean Composition** → Simple background, uncluttered, rule of thirds considered.
6. **No Brands or Logos** → Remove/avoid anything with text, logos, or trademarks.
7. **No People (or Release Attached)** → For first 3 submissions, avoid humans altogether.
8. **Natural Editing** → Avoid oversaturation, filters, or heavy HDR effects.
9. **Dust & Noise Check** → No dust spots, no ISO noise. Clean with editing tools if needed.
10. **Keywords Ready** → Write 10–20 accurate keywords + a clear title (e.g., "Fresh red apple on wooden table").

Other Platforms to Sell Your Photos

While iStockphoto is one of the oldest and most trusted marketplaces, it's not the only option. In fact, many successful photographers upload to **multiple stock platforms at once** to maximize exposure and sales. The more places your images live, the more chances you have to earn passive income from them.

1. Shutterstock

- **One of the biggest players** in the industry with millions of customers worldwide.
- Very contributor-friendly: anyone can apply, and approval is generally quicker than iStock.
- Payouts are lower per photo (often $0.25–$2 per download), but the sheer **volume of downloads** makes it worthwhile.
- Great platform for beginners since even simple, well-shot images (textures, everyday objects, nature) sell here.

2. Adobe Stock

- Directly tied to the **Adobe Creative Cloud ecosystem** (Photoshop, Illustrator, Premiere).
- Designers and creatives using Adobe apps can license your images seamlessly, so your photos are seen by a high-quality audience.
- Payouts are typically higher than Shutterstock (33% commission).
- Approval standards are strict but fair — if you're consistent, you'll build a strong passive income stream.

3. Alamy

- Known for **higher payouts per sale** ($20–$200+ per license).
- Focuses more on editorial and unique imagery (real-world scenes, street photography, travel).
- Slower sales volume compared to Shutterstock or Adobe, but when you make a sale, the payout can be significant.
- Great for photographers who enjoy travel, cityscapes, or documenting real life rather than just studio-style stock shots.

4. Other Options Worth Exploring

- **Dreamstime** → Smaller but solid marketplace. Good place to diversify.
- **Depositphotos** → Competitive payouts and frequent sales.
- **Getty Images** → Premium, highly selective version of iStock. If you get in, payouts can be excellent, but approval is tough.

Why You Should Upload Everywhere

Don't put all your photos in one basket. The effort of uploading to multiple platforms is usually just a few extra clicks, but the **income multiplies**. Many contributors report that their monthly revenue doubled or tripled once they started uploading beyond iStock.

A good workflow is:

1. Shoot → Edit → Export.
2. Upload the same batch of photos to Shutterstock, Adobe Stock, iStock, and Alamy.
3. Write one set of titles & keywords, then copy/paste across platforms.

That way, every photo you take is working for you on several fronts at once.

Earnings & Scaling in Digital Photography

1. What to Expect in the Beginning

- Most beginners start small.
- With just **10–20 approved photos** on iStock or Shutterstock, you might only see **$5–$20 per month** in downloads.
- That may not sound exciting, but remember: these earnings are *passive*. Once uploaded, your photos can keep selling for years without extra effort.

2. The Power of Portfolio Size

The single biggest factor in scaling your income is the **size and quality of your portfolio**.

- **100 photos** → $50–$200/month (typical for consistent contributors).
- **500 photos** → $200–$1,000/month, depending on subject matter.
- **1,000+ photos** → Many contributors in this range make **$2,000–$5,000+ per month**.

Some of the most dedicated contributors who treat stock photography like a real business (shooting daily, uploading thousands of images) report **$10,000+ monthly incomes**.

3. Smart Scaling: Workflows That Save Time

To scale efficiently:

1. **Batch shooting** → Don't take one-off shots; plan photo sessions with multiple usable images.
2. **Edit once, export many** → Apply consistent edits and export in different crops/aspects.
3. **Upload to multiple platforms** → iStock, Shutterstock, Adobe Stock, Alamy (same set of photos, multiple income streams).
4. **Reuse keywords/titles** → Keep a spreadsheet of keywords and copy them across platforms.

4. Niches That Sell Again and Again

Some subjects are *evergreen*—they never stop selling:

- **Business & Technology** (laptops, office, teamwork).
- **Health & Wellness** (fitness, food, doctors, mindfulness).
- **Nature & Landscapes** (beautiful but simple shots).
- **People & Lifestyle** (families, diversity, travel).

If you want to scale faster, focus on niches that *buyers need continuously*.

5. Turning Small Earnings into Serious Income

Think of stock photography like planting seeds:

- At first, you only see a sprout (a few dollars).
- But if you keep planting (uploading), your forest grows (hundreds of images working for you).
- After a year of consistent uploads, many contributors see exponential growth — **their older images keep earning while new ones add fresh income.**

That's why stock photography is a perfect fit for building **long-term passive income**.

6. Final Word on Scaling

Success doesn't come from uploading 10 photos and waiting. It comes from **treating this as a creative business**:

- Keep shooting.
- Keep uploading.
- Keep refining what works.

Over time, your portfolio becomes a digital asset — one that works for you 24/7, even while you sleep. And when combined with your other online income streams, it brings you closer to financial freedom.

Closing Inspiration

Digital photography isn't just about capturing beautiful moments — it's about creating assets that can work for you forever. Each photo you upload is like planting a seed in your financial garden. At first, it might seem small — a few downloads here, a few dollars there — but with consistency, your portfolio grows into a forest of passive income. And that's the key: not rushing, not giving up, but steadily building. Just like with any other online venture, success comes from patience, passion, and persistence. If you stay consistent, your camera can become more than a creative tool — it can become one of the stepping stones that carries you toward financial freedom.

6. Online Trading

When people think about making money online, they often picture selling products, running ads, or building an audience. But there's another way — one that doesn't require selling anything to anyone: **online trading**.

I've been involved in online trading since around 2006 or 2007, and I can tell you from personal experience — **it can be both exciting and rewarding**. However, it's also **risky** and **not for everyone**. If done without the right knowledge and discipline, it can quickly lead to losing your entire investment.

1. What Is Online Trading?

Online trading is simply buying and selling financial instruments — such as **stocks, currencies (Forex), commodities like gold and oil, cryptocurrencies, or indices** — through an online platform provided by a broker.

You aim to **buy low and sell high** (or sell high and buy low in short selling), making a profit from price movements. This can be done in minutes, hours, or over days and weeks, depending on your style.

2. The Reality of Risk

Let's be clear: **Trading is not a guaranteed income source**. For every trader who makes consistent profits, there are dozens who lose money.

The main reasons people fail are:

- **Lack of knowledge** — jumping in without truly understanding the markets.
- **No risk management** — risking too much on a single trade.
- **Emotional decisions** — letting fear or greed control trades instead of following a plan.

Rule #1: Never trade with money you can't afford to lose.

3. The Long Learning Curve

Becoming what I call a **"consistently profitable trader"** is rare because it takes:

- Months or even years of **study and practice**.
- The ability to follow a trading plan without emotional interference.
- A strong understanding of **risk control**.

Yes, there are countless free videos, articles, and courses online, but most are created by marketers, not real traders. They make money selling courses, not necessarily by trading successfully.

Professional traders rarely reveal everything they know, and even if they did, you'd still need **experience and practice** to make it work for you.

4. The Rewards If You Master It

Despite the challenges, **trading can be life-changing** if you approach it correctly. Once you develop the skills and discipline, you can:

- Work from anywhere with an internet connection.
- Trade in just a few hours a day (or less).
- Generate income without depending on customers, clients, or advertising.

But remember — **consistency is the goal**, not "getting rich quick."

5. How to Get Started (The Safe Way)

If you're interested in trading, here's how I recommend starting:

1. **Learn first** — study the basics of the markets you want to trade.
2. **Choose a reliable broker** — one that is regulated in a trusted country.
3. **Start with a demo account** — practice without risking real money.
4. **Learn risk management** — never risk more than 1–2% of your account on a single trade.
5. **Start small** — use the smallest trade size possible when moving to a live account.

6. Two Main Types of Trading: Day Trading vs. Swing Trading

When we talk about online trading, one important decision you'll face early on is:

How long do you want to hold your trades?

That's where the concepts of **day trading** and **swing trading** come in.

Day Trading

Day trading means **opening and closing your positions within the same day**.
You never hold trades overnight.

- **Goal:** Take advantage of short-term price movements — often lasting minutes to hours.
- **Time Commitment:** Requires you to be at your screen during active market hours.
- **Advantages:**
    - No overnight risk (you're not affected by overnight news or gaps).
    - Can generate daily profits if done well.
- **Disadvantages:**
    - Can be stressful because you need to make quick decisions.
    - Requires intense focus and discipline.

Day trading is fast-paced. It suits people who can handle quick thinking and don't mind spending several hours in front of the charts each day.

Swing Trading

Swing trading means **holding trades for several days, weeks, or even months** — as long as the trend remains in your favor.

- **Goal:** Capture bigger moves in the market over a longer period.
- **Time Commitment:** Doesn't require watching the charts all day; you can check the markets once or twice a day.
- **Advantages:**
    - Less stressful than day trading.
    - You can combine it with a full-time job or other business.
- **Disadvantages:**
    - You are exposed to overnight risks (news, price gaps).
    - Profits take longer to realize.

Swing trading is slower and calmer, making it a better fit for those who want to trade part-time or alongside other work.

Which Is Better?

Neither is "better" — it's all about your **personality, schedule, and tolerance for risk**.

- If you like **fast action** and can focus for hours, you might enjoy day trading.
- If you prefer a **slower pace** and don't mind holding trades for days, swing trading could be better.

Some traders even combine both — swing trading larger trends while day trading smaller opportunities in between. This is what I recommend as well, because it's the approach I personally follow. I will explain how.

Trading vs. Investing — Understanding the Difference

Many beginners confuse **trading** with **investing**, but they are two very different approaches to making money in the markets.

Investing is the process of buying assets — such as stocks, ETFs, real estate investment trusts, or even businesses — with the intention of holding them for years or decades. The goal is to benefit from **long-term growth** and possibly receive **passive income** along the way (like dividends or rental income). Investing requires patience and often ignores short-term price movements, focusing instead on the bigger picture over time.

Trading, on the other hand, is much more **active**. Traders buy and sell assets within shorter time frames — sometimes in minutes (day trading), sometimes over a few days or weeks (swing trading). The goal is to profit from **short-term price changes** rather than waiting years for the investment to grow. Trading requires constant attention, market analysis, and strict risk management.

To put it simply:

- **Investors** aim to **build wealth slowly** over many years.
- **Traders** aim to **extract profits quickly** by taking advantage of short-term opportunities.

Both can be profitable, but trading demands more skill, discipline, and emotional control — and it carries higher risk if done without proper knowledge.

How to Start Practicing Trading Without Risk

One of the biggest mistakes beginners make is jumping straight into the markets with real money before they've learned the basics or developed a winning strategy. This almost always leads to losses — not because trading doesn't work, but because they treated it like a lottery ticket instead of a skill to be mastered.

The safest and smartest way to start is by using a **demo account** (also called a **paper trading account**).
A demo account allows you to trade with **virtual money** in a real market environment. You see the same prices, charts, and market movements as live traders, but there's zero risk to your wallet.

Here's how to start practicing risk-free:

1. **Choose a reputable broker** — Pick one that offers both demo and live accounts, has a good reputation, and is regulated by a respected financial authority.
2. **Open a demo account** — It usually takes minutes. The broker will give you a set amount of virtual funds to trade with.
3. **Use real strategies** — Don't just "play around" with random trades. Treat the demo as if it's real money. This will train you to follow rules and manage risks.
4. **Practice risk management** — Never risk more than a small percentage of your account on a single trade, even in demo mode. The habit will carry over to live trading.
5. **Track your performance** — Keep a trading journal of your wins, losses, and what you learned from each trade.

Remember: your goal in demo trading is **not** to see how much virtual money you can make, but to prove that you can trade **consistently and profitably over time** without reckless risk-taking.

Once you can show consistent profits in a demo account for at least **three to six months**, you can begin trading with real money — starting small and scaling up only as your skills grow.

Common Mistakes to Avoid as a Beginner Trader

Many beginners lose money in trading not because the markets are impossible to beat, but because they repeat the same avoidable mistakes. Knowing these pitfalls in advance can save you years of frustration — and potentially thousands of dollars.

1. Trading Without a Plan
Jumping into trades without a clear strategy is like sailing without a map. Every successful trader has a plan that defines *when* to enter, *when* to exit, and *how much* to risk. Without this, you're just gambling.

2. Risking Too Much on a Single Trade
A single bad trade should never wipe out your account. Many beginners risk 20–50% of their capital at once, hoping for a big win. Smart traders risk only **1–2%** per trade, preserving their account for the long run.

3. Overtrading
The more trades you take, the more you expose yourself to risk. Beginners often trade out of boredom or excitement, instead of waiting for high-probability setups. Remember: sometimes the best trade is **no trade at all**.

4. Letting Losses Run
Holding onto losing positions "hoping they'll come back" is one of the fastest ways to drain your account. Professional traders set **stop-loss orders** and accept small losses quickly before they turn into disasters.

5. Ignoring Risk Management
Risk management is more important than strategy. Even with an average system, disciplined risk control can keep you profitable over time. Without it, even the best system will fail.

6. Trading Based on Emotions
Fear and greed are a trader's worst enemies. They lead to revenge trading after a loss or jumping into trades without analysis. The key is to stay calm, follow your plan, and avoid impulsive decisions.

7. Switching Strategies Too Often
Many beginners abandon a strategy after a few losing trades, constantly hopping to the "next best thing." All strategies have losing streaks — the key is to stick with one long enough to truly master it.

How Should You Trade?

Now that you have a clear understanding of what trading is and how it works, you might be asking:

"Okay, I know what trading is… but how should I actually trade?"

First of all, take to heart everything I emphasized earlier — especially the part about **demo trading** for at least **3–6 months**. Your first goal is not to make money; it's to prove to yourself that you can trade consistently and profitably *without risk*. Only when you have achieved consistent profitability in your demo account should you even think about trading with real money.

Second, even when you make the switch to real money, start with **a small account**. It doesn't matter if you have a large sum in your bank — treat your first live trading capital as an extension of your practice. This is where you train yourself to handle the **psychological pressure** of real money on the line, which is a completely different experience from demo trading.

Third, whether you're trading a small account or you've built it up over time, never risk more than **1–2%** of your trading capital on a single position. This rule protects you from the inevitable losing streaks and keeps your account alive long enough for your edge to play out.

Day Trading, Swing Trading or Both?

As I mentioned before, I recommend doing both **day trading** and **swing trading** if you can — and if your schedule allows it. However, you don't have to do both at the same time. Day trading requires you to sit at your computer for several hours each day, closely monitoring the market. Swing trading, on the other hand, does not require constant screen time.

With this in mind, you can decide whether you want to do both or focus only on swing trading, depending on your lifestyle and daily schedule.

Another important point is that **this trading section is directly linked to the next chapter**, which will focus on making your active income generate **passive income** for you.

As I explained back in Chapter 2 on financial freedom:

1. **First**, you must create at least one strong source of active income — using methods I've already covered, such as running a website, YouTubing, and others.
2. **Then**, take a portion of that active income and use it to generate passive income.

Trading — along with investing (which I'll cover later) — are two of the key ways to transform your active income into passive income. Of course, day trading itself is **not** passive income, since it requires active daily work. But swing trading, along with other forms of investing, can be structured so that your money works for you even when you're not working.

What Is the Optimum Time to Buy and Sell?

Trading is all about buying and selling. Online trading is no different — except you use your computer or phone to buy and sell through the Internet against other market participants. There are many ways to decide when to buy or sell. Entire libraries of books, articles, and videos exist on this topic.

But this book is meant to be practical, not an encyclopedia. So instead of explaining all possible methods, I'll focus on the way *I* trade — what has worked for me and still works today. Even if you are completely new to online trading, you've likely seen a price chart on the news when they talk about the stock market, currencies, cryptocurrencies, metals, or commodities. The chart shows the market's movement and whether prices have gone up or down. Analysts then give their opinion on where the market may go next.

My approach is based on analyzing the price chart to decide when to buy or sell. There are many chart types, but here I will focus on the one that has consistently helped me — not because others don't exist, but because I don't want to overload you with useless complexity.

I've seen many people spend years studying different trading strategies, techniques, and indicators without ever making money. Some read chart analysis books with over 5,000 pages, yet still lose when they trade. Why? Because they can't apply what they've learned in the real market. Theory alone won't make you profitable.

So, let's be straightforward and focus on what works. I won't explain every charting method, because they can seem complicated and take years to master. Instead, I'll narrow the focus to a specific price chart element that I believe is the most powerful: **Candlesticks**.

Candlesticks are the only real-time indicators that show you where the market is most likely to move next. All the other colorful, sophisticated, and "fascinating" indicators people pile onto their charts are lagging, misleading, and often drain your money instead of making it grow.

Let's start here: **What are candlesticks?**

What Are Candlesticks and How to Read Them

Candlesticks are one of the most important tools in trading, and they are far more than just colorful shapes on a chart. Each candlestick represents a period of market activity — it could be one minute, five minutes, an hour, a day, or any time frame you choose.

A candlestick shows four key pieces of information:

1. **Opening price** – where the market started during that time period.
2. **Closing price** – where the market ended during that time period.
3. **Highest price** – the peak price reached during that period.
4. **Lowest price** – the lowest price reached during that period.

The "body" of the candlestick shows the range between the opening and closing prices. If the close is higher than the open, the candlestick is usually green (or white or gray), meaning the market moved upward during that period. If the close is lower than the open, it's usually red (or black), meaning the market moved downward.

The thin lines above and below the body are called "wicks" or "shadows," and they represent the highs and lows of that period. Together, these elements create a visual snapshot of market sentiment — who's in control, buyers or sellers, and how strong their momentum is.

Candlestick charts are powerful because they give you this information at a glance, without the delay and confusion that comes with many technical indicators. They reflect real-time market psychology, showing you when traders are optimistic, fearful, or uncertain.

Here's your example showing a gray (bullish) candlestick and a black (bearish) candlestick side-by-side, with each of their four key prices — Open, Close, High, and Low — clearly marked. This should visually help your readers understand the basic structure before you introduce the strongest candlestick patterns later:

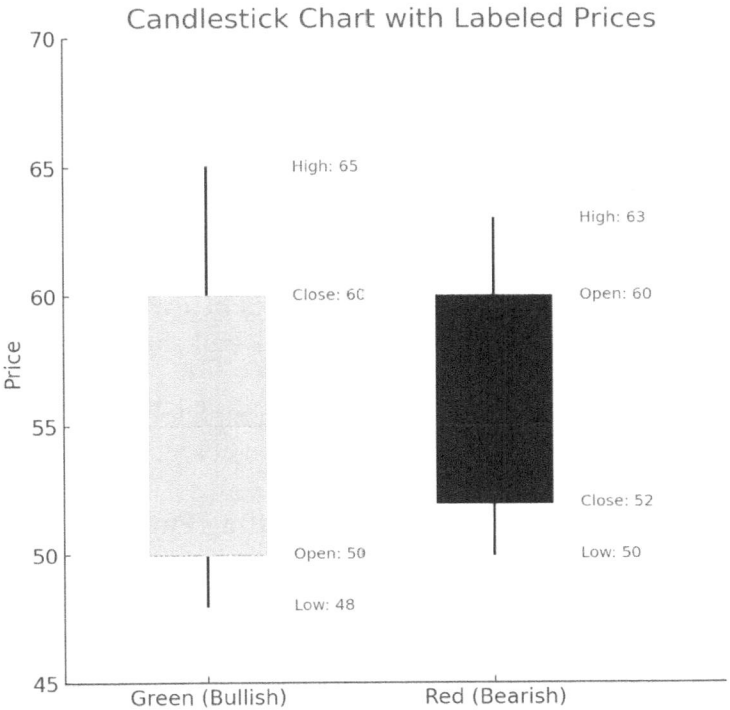

Over time, traders noticed that certain shapes or sequences of candlesticks tend to appear before the market moves in a particular direction. These are called **candlestick signals** or **patterns**. Some patterns suggest a trend will continue, while others indicate a possible reversal.

There are dozens — even hundreds — of candlestick patterns that you could study. But learning them all is not only overwhelming, it's unnecessary. Most of them have low success rates or work only in specific market conditions.

In this book, I will focus only on the strongest candlestick patterns — the ones with the highest probability of success and the lowest risk. Mastering a few powerful setups is far better than trying to memorize every pattern you see in a textbook:

1. Bearish Engulfing Pattern and Dark Cloud Cover

When analyzing candlesticks, one of the most important reversal signals you'll encounter is the **Bearish Engulfing Pattern**. This pattern usually forms at the top of an uptrend and warns traders that the bullish move may be coming to an end.

A Bearish Engulfing happens when:

1. A gray (bullish) candlestick forms during an uptrend.
2. The next candlestick opens higher than the previous close, but then sellers step in with strength.
3. The bearish (black) candlestick closes **below the midpoint or even below the body** of the previous bullish candlestick.

This "engulfing" action shows that sellers completely took control, overpowering buyers who were previously in charge.

Here's a simple graph of the **Bearish Engulfing Pattern**:

- On the left, you see the **bullish candle** (gray), where the market closed higher than it opened.
- On the right, you see the **bearish candle** (black), which completely engulfs the body of the bullish candle, signaling a possible reversal.

This is exactly how the pattern looks on a chart:

- **Candle 1 (Gray):** Market is moving up, optimism is present.
- **Candle 2 (Black):** Opens higher but then closes much lower than the previous candle's open, showing strong selling pressure.

This engulfing action — especially when the second candle is **large and decisive** — is what makes this pattern powerful:

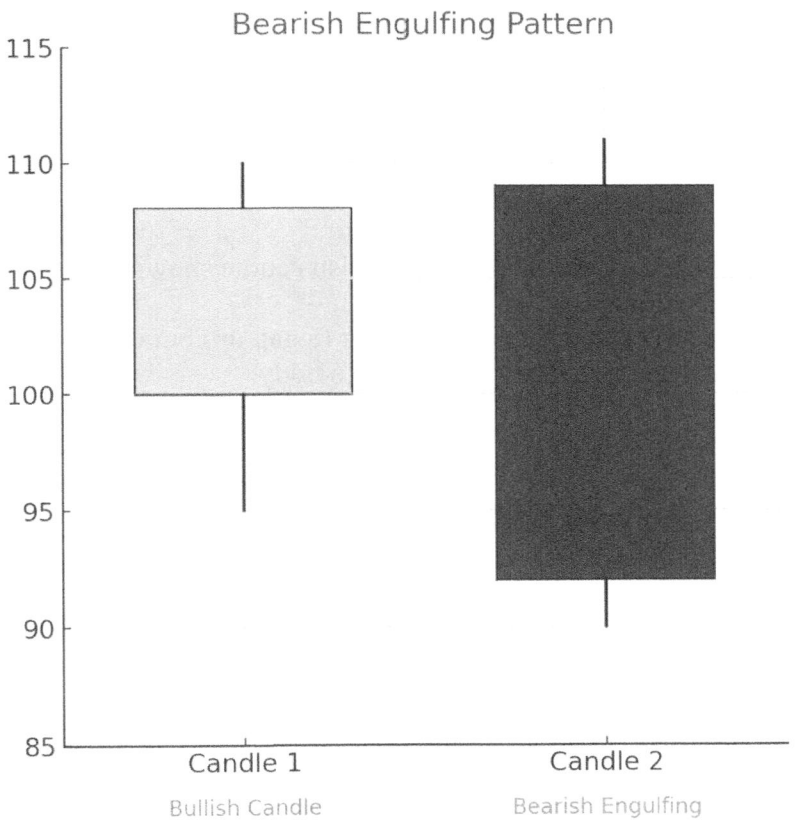

The Dark Cloud Cover

A very powerful variation of the Bearish Engulfing is the **Dark Cloud Cover** pattern.

- It appears after a series of bullish candlesticks at the top of an uptrend.

- The bearish candlestick opens above the high or close of the previous bullish candlestick, creating the illusion that the uptrend will continue.
- But instead of rising, the market reverses — the candlestick closes deep into the body of the previous bullish candle, forming a "dark cloud" over the buyers' optimism.

This sudden reversal often shocks traders who expected the bull market to continue, which is why the Dark Cloud Cover is considered one of the strongest bearish reversal signals.

Here's the chart illustrating the **Dark Cloud Cover** pattern. It shows how the bearish candle (black) opens above the previous bullish candle's close but then drops deep into its body — signaling a potential strong reversal:

- **Candle 1 (Gray):** A strong bullish candle showing upward momentum.
- **Candle 2 (Black):** Opens higher (a gap up) but closes well below the midpoint of Candle 1's body.

The deeper the black candle pushes into the gray candle, the stronger the reversal signal. Traders usually ignore small or weak ones, waiting only for **big, powerful patterns** to reduce risk.

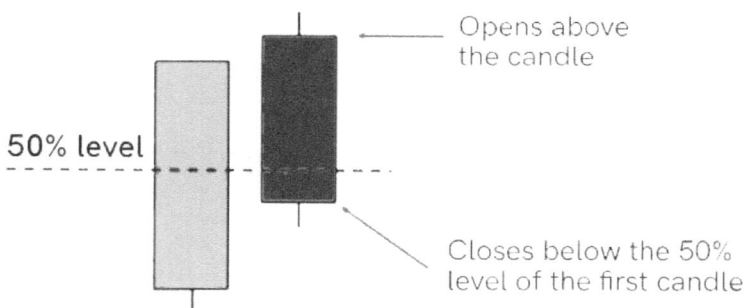

The Importance of Size

The **size of the bearish candlestick** is what makes the difference between a weak signal and a strong one:

- **Small bearish candles** that barely push into the bullish body are unreliable and often lead to false signals.
- **Large bearish candles** that cut deep — especially when they close below the midpoint of the previous candle — show that sellers have gained real control.

The bigger the bearish candlestick in the Dark Cloud Cover pattern, the **stronger the reversal signal** at the top of a bull market.

How to Reduce Risk

To trade safer and with more confidence:

- **Ignore small or weak patterns.** They are easily invalidated.
- **Wait for big, obvious patterns.** When the bearish candlestick is large and clear, the success rate of the pattern is higher, and the risk of being trapped is lower.

This patience alone saves traders from many unnecessary losses.

In short: The Bearish Engulfing — especially in the form of a strong Dark Cloud Cover — is one of the clearest warning signs that a bullish trend is about to reverse. But the **size** of the bearish candlestick is the key factor. The bigger it is, the stronger the signal.

How to Trade Using Bearish Engulfing Patterns

In the chart below, which comes from gold's 5-minute timeframe, you can see several Bearish Engulfing Patterns — some of which are also Dark Cloud Cover patterns. Almost in the middle of the chart, I've highlighted a Dark Cloud Cover, which is my favorite setup to sell.

Here's how to trade it step by step:

1. **Entry** – You sell at the close of the black candlestick that forms the Dark Cloud Cover pattern.
2. **Stop Loss** – Place your stop loss just a little above the high price of that same bearish candlestick.
3. **Take Profit (Target)** – A simple and effective approach is to set your target as large as the size of that strong bearish

candlestick which created the pattern. The bigger the candlestick, the stronger the signal, and usually the better the potential profit.

Don't worry if you're not yet familiar with terms like *stop loss*, *target* and *timeframe*. I'll explain these in detail later, along with another important concept: in online trading, you can **sell even before you buy** something. This might sound strange at first, but it's a standard part of how trading works in modern markets — and I'll make it clear when we get there.

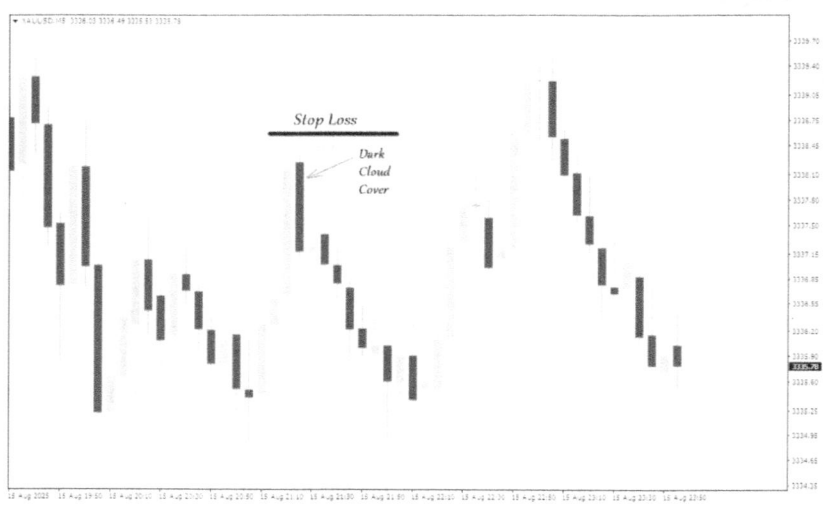

Now that I have shared a signal that shows how a trade works, it is the right time to explain a few important terms before introducing the next strong candlestick pattern.

Stop Loss

A *stop loss* is a safety net. It is a price level you set in advance that automatically closes your trade if the market moves against you. Why is this important? Because no matter how good a pattern looks, no signal is 100% guaranteed. The stop loss protects your trading account by limiting your loss to a manageable amount. For example, if you sell based on a bearish pattern and the market suddenly keeps moving higher instead of dropping, your stop loss will close the trade before it gets too painful. This is how professional traders stay in the game for the long run.

Target (Take Profit)

A *target* or *take profit* is the opposite of a stop loss. It is a price level you set in advance that automatically closes your trade when the market moves in your favor and reaches your goal. This ensures you lock in your profit without letting greed push you to stay in too long. If your candlestick signal suggests a strong downward move, your target can be set at a logical point — such as the same distance as the size of the candlestick that gave the signal, or sometimes more if the market trend is strong.

In short:

- Stop Loss = protect yourself from losing too much.
- Target = secure your profits when the market has moved enough in your favor.

Timeframes

When traders analyze charts, they can look at different *timeframes*. A timeframe is simply how much time each candlestick represents. For example:

- On a **5-minute chart**, *(like the gold chart I shared)* each candlestick shows how price moved within 5 minutes.
- On a **1-hour chart**, each candlestick shows one hour of price movement.
- On a **daily chart**, each candlestick represents a full day.

The choice of timeframe depends on your trading style:

- **Day traders** usually prefer smaller timeframes like 1-minute, 5-minute, or 15-minute charts because they want quick trades.
- **Swing traders** often use 1-hour, 4-hour, or daily charts because they want to capture bigger moves that last days or weeks.

For example, the *gold 5-minute chart* I showed earlier is great for spotting quick trades during the day. But if you only have time to check markets once or twice a day, you may prefer the daily chart.

Entry

The *entry* is simply the exact price point where you open a trade. In other words, it's the moment you officially "get in" to the market, whether buying or selling.

Your entry is extremely important because it determines both your potential profit and your risk. A bad entry (too early or too late) can turn a winning signal into a losing trade.

In the **gold 5-minute chart** example I shared earlier, the entry happens **right at the close of the bearish (black) candlestick** that forms the Dark Cloud Cover pattern. Since the next candlestick opens at the same price, it means your entry is at the **open of the next candlestick** immediately after the pattern has completed.

This is the safest way to enter: you wait until the bearish candlestick is fully closed (so the signal is confirmed) before entering the trade. Jumping in before a candlestick closes is risky, because it can still change shape and cancel the pattern.

So to summarize:

- **Entry** = the price where you open the trade.
- In this strategy, you enter at the *close of the bearish candlestick* that forms the Dark Cloud Cover, which is also the open of the next candlestick.

Now, let's move on to the second group of candlestick patterns that I rely on and trust the most:

2. Bullish Engulfing Pattern and Piercing Line

The **Bullish Engulfing Pattern** is one of the strongest reversal signals in candlestick trading. It typically forms at the bottom of a downtrend and signals that buyers are taking control.

- **How it forms:**
    - A small bearish (black) candlestick appears first, showing selling pressure.
    - Then, a larger bullish (gray) candlestick follows that completely "engulfs" the body of the black one.
    - This shows that buyers not only reversed the prior selling but also overpowered it strongly.

- **What it means:**
This pattern indicates a potential shift from a bearish trend to a bullish one. The bigger and stronger the bullish candlestick, the stronger the signal. Just like in bearish setups, it's best to ignore weak and tiny patterns and focus only on big, clear signals to reduce risk.

- **How to trade it:**
    - **Entry:** At the close of the bullish engulfing candlestick (or the open of the next one).
    - **Stop Loss:** Just below the low of the bullish candlestick.
    - **Target:** At least the size of the bullish candlestick, but often more, since bullish engulfing patterns can start much larger uptrends.

Piercing Line Pattern

The **Piercing Line** is a special type of bullish engulfing signal, but slightly weaker than the full engulfing. It's still powerful when it forms in the right spot (at the end of a downtrend).

- **How it forms:**
    - A bearish (black) candlestick appears first, continuing the downtrend.
    - Then, a bullish (gray) candlestick follows that opens lower but closes at least **above the midpoint** of the previous black candle's body.
    - Unlike the full engulfing, it doesn't need to cover the entire black body — but piercing halfway already shows strong buying pressure.

- **What it means:**
The Piercing Line signals that sellers tried to push lower, but

buyers stepped in with strength and reclaimed more than half the ground in one move. This often marks the beginning of a bullish reversal.
- **How to trade it:**
    - **Entry:** At the close of the bullish candlestick.
    - **Stop Loss:** Just below its low.
    - **Target:** Equal to the bullish candle's size or more, depending on market conditions.

Key Point: Just as with bearish patterns, **size matters.** A big, bold bullish engulfing or piercing line means real strength from buyers. Small, weak ones can easily fail, so patience pays off.

In the next chart, you'll notice several **Bullish Engulfing Patterns.** This pattern forms when a small black candle is completely swallowed by a larger gray candle, signaling a potential reversal to the upside. Here's how you trade it step by step:

1. **Identify the Pattern**
   Look for a small bearish (black) candlestick followed immediately by a larger bullish (gray) candlestick that fully engulfs the black one.
2. **Confirm the Signal**
   Make sure the gray candle closes above the open of the previous black candle. The stronger and larger the gray candle, the more reliable the signal.
3. **Entry Point**
   Enter a buy position at the **close of the bullish candlestick** (or at the open of the next candle). This is where the reversal momentum begins.
4. **Stop Loss Placement**
   Place your stop loss slightly below the **lowest price** of the bullish candlestick that formed the pattern. This protects you in case the reversal fails.
5. **Take Profit (Target)**
   Set your target at least equal to the size (height) of the bullish candlestick. For example, if the bullish candle is 10 points tall, your take profit should be 10 points above your entry price.

Remember: Bullish Engulfing Patterns tell you to **buy**, whereas Bearish Engulfing Patterns tell you to **sell**. Following this step-by-step process helps you minimize risk while taking advantage of market reversals:

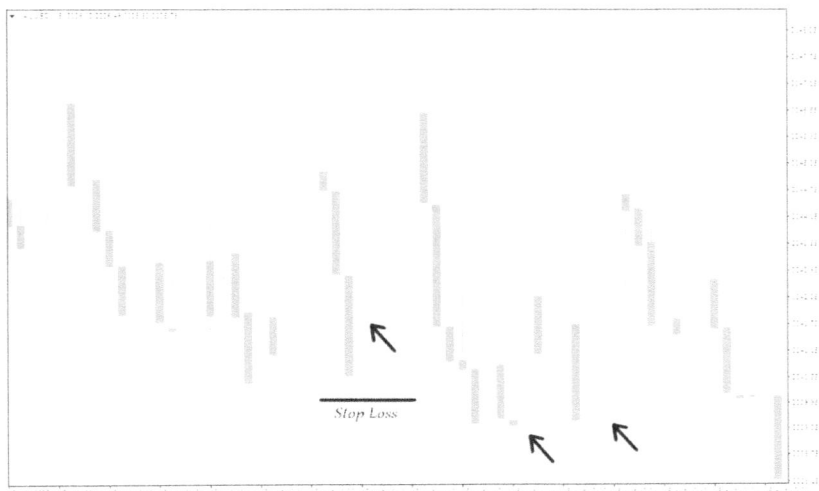

On the gold **1-hour chart** below, you can see a **Piercing Line Pattern**. This is another bullish reversal signal *(a variation of Bullish Engulfing)* that often appears at the bottom of a downtrend. Here's how you trade it step by step:

1. **Identify the Pattern**
    - The first candle is bearish (black) and closes lower.
    - The second candle is bullish (gray) and **opens below** the black candle's close. but then pushes upward and closes at least halfway into the body of the black candle.

    This "piercing" action shows that buyers are stepping in and overpowering sellers.

2. **Confirm the Signal**
   Make sure the bullish candle closes **well into the body** of the previous black candle (ideally above its midpoint). The deeper the penetration, the stronger the reversal signal.

3. **Entry Point**
   Enter a buy trade at the **close of the bullish candle** that formed the Piercing Line pattern (which is also the open of the next

candle).

4. **Stop Loss Placement**
   Place your stop loss slightly **below the lowest price** of the bullish candle in the Piercing Line. This keeps your risk controlled if the pattern fails.

5. **Take Profit (Target)**
   Your closest target can be set at a distance **equal to the length of the bullish candle** that formed the Piercing Line. This means if the candle is 15 points tall, you place your target 15 points above your entry.

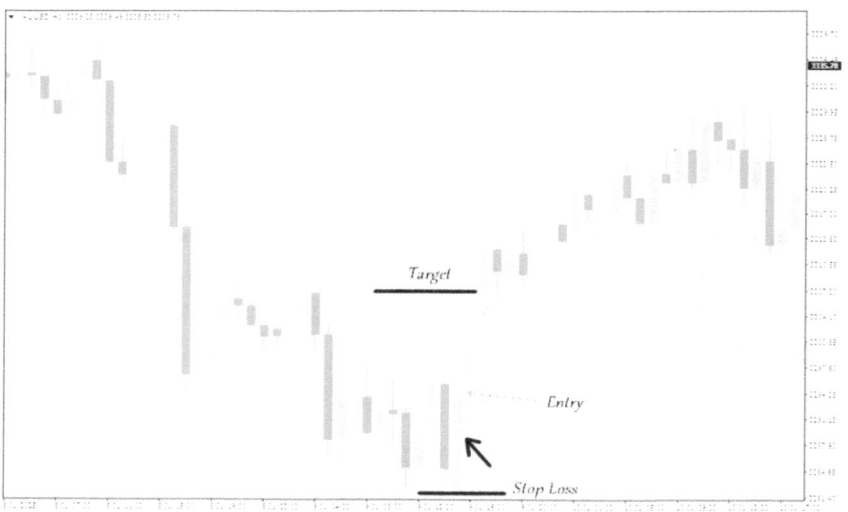

Important Note: There are dozens of bullish candlestick reversal signals. But like with the bearish ones, you should **ignore weak and small patterns** and only act on the **big, clear ones**. The bigger the bullish candle compared to the black one before it, the lower your risk and the higher your chance of success.

Final Notes About Trading

1. The methods I have shown you here are based on the **strongest candlestick patterns**. These signals are:

- Easier for beginners to identify on charts.

- More reliable compared to weaker patterns.
- Less risky when traded correctly.
- Higher in probability of success if you follow the steps exactly.

There are **hundreds of other candlestick patterns** in trading literature, but I purposely left them out. Trying to memorize and use too many patterns will only overwhelm you, confuse you, and cause costly mistakes.

There are also advanced **chart analysis techniques** that go far beyond candlesticks. Many of these require years of practice, and even then, most traders fail to profit from them. That's why I didn't bring them into this book.

This book is written to be **practical and profitable**, not encyclopedic. If I tried to cover everything, this book would become thousands of pages long — something you might never finish. Even if you did, it would probably not help you make money. In fact, it might make you lose by drowning you in theory instead of teaching you what really works.

Trading can be highly profitable if you approach it the right way: start simple, master the strongest signals, practice on demo accounts, and then gradually move into live trading with discipline and consistency.

Trading, on its own, can be a powerful way to make money. But remember: it is only one part of your bigger journey toward **financial freedom**. The real key is to take the income you earn actively — whether from trading, running a business, or another source — and use a portion of it to create **passive income** streams.

This is where trading connects directly with the next chapter. Day trading may give you active income, but swing trading and long-term investing are the bridges that allow your money to start working for you. That is how you move closer, step by step, to the financial freedom you deserve.

2. You can easily find more information about the patterns I've explained by searching the internet. There are thousands of articles and videos about them. But here is the truth: **don't go beyond what I've shared with you here.**

Why? Because it doesn't work. I've learned this the hard way.

Even after years of trading, I still rely on the same candlestick patterns I've shown you in this book, plus just a handful of other candlestick and technical analysis patterns. I ignore all the rest because I've tested them and discovered that they carry far more risk and simply aren't worth considering.

When I meet with other traders, they often talk about the new chart patterns or fancy strategies they're experimenting with. I listen politely — but I never try them. Why? Because I've already been burned enough by chasing every "new thing." I finally learned that if a strategy is working, you don't abandon it. You stick with it, master it, and refine it.

The temptation to "find a better way" or to "take shortcuts" is strong. Many traders believe that if they learn more patterns, they'll find more trade setups and make more money. But the reality is just the opposite: this mindset almost always leads to losses.

You cannot force the market to hand you profits. Your job is to wait patiently for the market to form a **strong, reliable setup** — then trade it with discipline. Jumping from one strategy to another, or trying to juggle too many approaches at once, is nothing but a waste of time and money.

3. Now that I've mentioned "other traders," let me share an important secret with you: **it's extremely rare to find a truly consistently profitable trader.** And even if you do, the chances that they'll openly share their methods with you are almost zero.

Here's why:

- The traders who are really profitable are usually quiet, humble, and introverted. They don't brag about their results, and they don't feel the need to prove themselves.

- On the other hand, the traders who are losing most of the time are often the loudest. They talk about their "skills," their "discoveries," and their so-called "systems."

When they happen to get lucky and make a profit, they shout it from the rooftops. But when they lose — which is most of the time — they go silent. They trade like gamblers. If they get lucky and double their account by taking reckless risks, they let everyone know. But the following week, when they wipe out that same account, they disappear until their next lucky streak.

Spending time with these kinds of traders can be dangerous. Why? Because it can make you feel like you're the one failing, while "everyone else" is making millions. But this is an illusion created by dishonest or attention-seeking people.

Avoid them. Ignore their noise. Stick to your own plan.

Remember, your goal is not to double your account every month. The people who chase that dream almost always end up losing everything the next month — or even the next week.

Your real goal is to become a **consistently profitable trader** — someone who ends each month with steady profits, even if it's just 5%. That small, reliable gain, repeated month after month, will compound into something extraordinary over time.

Don't let flashy, histrionic people ruin your trading journey. Stay patient. Stay disciplined. Stay focused on your own strategy.

4. Although I've already mentioned this earlier, I must repeat it again because it's **extremely important**: **never trade without a stop loss.**

Think of trading without a stop loss like driving on a highway without brakes — it might feel fine for a while, but sooner or later, disaster will strike.

Here's why:

- Sometimes, when you trade without a stop loss and the market goes against you, it might eventually turn around and let you

escape at breakeven or even with some profit. This seems like a "lucky break," but in reality, it's a **bad teacher**. It tricks you into repeating the same mistake.
- But luck doesn't last forever. One day, the market won't turn around. It will keep going against you until your account is wiped out.

Some traders make an even worse mistake: when their trade goes against them and they don't have a stop loss, they **add to the losing position** — this is called "averaging down."

- Occasionally, they get lucky, and the market turns in their favor, letting them close with a profit.
- But one day, it won't. And when that happens, the account will blow up completely, often wiping out not only the current balance but also all the profits they had worked hard to build.

Trading is not gambling. Trading is not a lottery ticket.

Trading is a **long-term business**. You're not here to make a quick buck and walk away. You're here to learn how to make money consistently, year after year, for the rest of your life. That's why discipline matters more than luck.

So, don't fall into the traps that destroy traders:

- Never trade without a stop loss.
- Never average down on a losing position.
- Never rely on luck.

Stay disciplined, follow your plan, and protect your capital at all costs.

5. This is also something I already mentioned before, but it's so important that I must emphasize it again: **do not start trading with real money.**

Here's the correct path to follow:

1. **Open a demo account that matches your future real account size.**
   - If you plan to open a $1,000 real account later, then open a $1,000 demo account now.
   - Don't open a $100,000 demo account if you won't ever trade that much in reality — it will give you the wrong impression.
2. **Treat the demo account as if it were your hard-earned money.**
   - Don't think "it's just demo money."
   - Force yourself to be disciplined. Wait for the real, strong trade setups or signals.
3. **Stay in demo trading until you are consistently profitable.**
   - Give yourself at least **3 to 6 months** of consistent profit on your demo account.
   - Only then move to real trading.
4. **Open your real account with the same amount you practiced with.**
   - If your demo was $1,000, then open a $1,000 live account.
   - Don't add extra money. Start small.
5. **Grow slowly and steadily.**
   - Your goal is not to get rich overnight.
   - With consistency, your account will grow into something reasonably big that produces serious income.

Remember, trading is a marathon, not a sprint. Those who try to rush almost always fail. But if you grow step by step, you'll have the discipline and experience to succeed long-term.

6. Maybe you already have a lot of savings. Maybe your business makes plenty of money. That's great. But no matter how much money you have, **never start trading with a big real account**.

Here's why:

- **Trading with real money triggers emotions.**
  Even if you know all the rules and strategies, once your hard-earned money is on the line, fear and greed kick in. These emotions are extremely difficult for beginners to control.

- **The bigger the money, the stronger the emotions.**
  If you risk too much too soon, your decisions will be driven by panic or excitement instead of discipline and logic.
- **Let the natural process work.**
  Start small. Grow your account slowly as your skills improve. Don't try to take shortcuts by throwing big money into the market — it will almost always end badly.

Trading is not about how much you start with. It's about how consistently you can grow. Even a small account can become big over time if you manage it with discipline.

7. Avoid Training Courses, Signal Services, and Fake Money Managers.

This point is extremely important, and I want to emphasize it clearly: stay away from trading courses, market analysis services, signal providers, and so-called money managers.

- **Trading courses:**
  Almost all trading courses are taught by people who have never been consistently profitable traders themselves. Real profitable traders don't sell courses — they don't need to. They make their money from trading, not from teaching beginners.
- **Market analysis and signal services:**
  These are nothing more than scams. Not only are they run by people who cannot trade, but in many countries — including the United States and Canada — they are illegal. If you buy their signals, you won't make money. In fact, you will lose money because you are following the blind.
- **So-called money managers:**
  Beware of people who ask you to invest with them, promising monthly profits. A real professional trader doesn't need your money and doesn't want the headache of dealing with investors. In many cases, these schemes are **illegal money management operations** that eventually collapse into Ponzi schemes — if they weren't one from the very beginning.

If you want to succeed in trading, don't look for shortcuts through courses, signals, or money managers. **Rely on your own skills, your own discipline, and your own trading plan.**

8. Another critical piece of advice is this: **choose one market to focus on and master it.**

Many beginners make the mistake of spreading themselves too thin. They keep too many charts open, trying to monitor multiple markets at the same time. This creates confusion, distraction, and poor decision-making. Trading doesn't reward the one who watches the most screens; it rewards the one who masters a single market with discipline and patience.

If you ask me which markets are the best to focus on, my answer is clear: **indices like the S&P 500 or metals like gold.**

- **Indices (like the S&P 500):**
  These markets are linked to real businesses and the strongest economy in the world — the United States. Their movements are based on real economic activity, corporate performance, and global financial flows. That makes them more reliable and logical compared to other markets. Personally, I prefer indices, especially the S&P 500, because of this strong connection to reality.
- **Metals (like gold):**
  Gold is also a powerful and reliable market with deep liquidity. It reacts strongly to global economic conditions, inflation, and investor sentiment.

By contrast, **currencies (forex)** often move in unpredictable ways, with little logic or boundaries. They are heavily influenced by speculation, central bank actions, and political events. While some traders do focus on forex, I don't recommend it for beginners.

Pick one strong market — like the S&P 500 or gold — and devote yourself to mastering it. This focus will give you much more clarity and consistency compared to chasing every possible opportunity across dozens of markets.

9. Another important point to clarify is **time frames**. I've already explained what they are, but now let's connect them directly to your trading style.

- **Day Trading:**
  If you want to be a day trader, you should focus on short time frames, like the **5-minute chart**. These allow you to spot setups, open positions, and close them within the same day. Day trading requires focus and screen time, but it gives you multiple opportunities during a single trading session.
- **Swing Trading:**
  If you prefer holding your positions for longer — sometimes several days or even weeks — you should use higher time frames, such as the **1-hour chart** or longer. These give you a bigger picture of the market and help you ride stronger price movements without needing to sit in front of the screen all day.

It's completely up to you whether you want to be a day trader or a swing trader. Personally, I do both. I take some short-term day trades, but I also hold certain positions for longer when the market gives me a strong setup.

Later, in the section on **generating passive income and investment**, I will explain more about holding positions longer — especially as part of building wealth and financial freedom.

The key is to choose a time frame that fits your personality and lifestyle. If you have several hours a day to dedicate, day trading might work for you. If not, swing trading is a great option. What matters is consistency and sticking to the plan.

10. Your **trading platform** is also very important. This is the software you use to analyze charts and place trades.

- My personal favorite is **MetaTrader 4 (MT4)**.
  MT4 is simple, professional, and extremely reliable. Most brokers support it, and it has been the standard for traders worldwide for many years.
- Many brokers also offer **web-based platforms**, but in my experience, these are usually less professional, harder to work with, and not as flexible as MT4.

For your learning and long-term consistency, I strongly recommend using MT4. It has everything you need to read candlestick patterns, set entries, stop losses, and targets, and manage your trades efficiently.

When you sign up for an account with a broker, you'll find instructions on their website about where to download and install their MT4 platform. If you don't see it right away, simply send them a message and ask — they will guide you to the download page.

11. One of the golden rules of trading is this: **never risk more than 1–2% of your trading capital on a single trade.**

- **What does this mean?**
  If a trade goes against you and hits the stop loss, you should lose no more than 1–2% of your account balance.
- **Example:**
  Suppose your account balance is **$1,000**.
    - 1% of $1,000 = **$10**
    - 2% of $1,000 = **$20**

  This means that if your trade hits the stop loss, your loss should be limited to **$10–$20 only**.

- **Target (Take Profit):**
  Your target can be:
    - Equal to the stop loss (a **1x reward-to-risk ratio**), or
    - Twice the stop loss (a **2x reward-to-risk ratio**).

  In the same $1,000 account example:

    - If your stop loss is $20 and you set a 1x target, you make $20 if the market hits your target.
    - If you set a 2x target, you make $40 when the market hits your target.

For beginners, I strongly recommend starting with **1x targets**. This builds confidence, helps you get used to consistency, and reduces the emotional pressure of waiting too long.

⚠ Don't be fooled by what some so-called traders say about holding trades until making **x10 or x15 profit**. That's unrealistic for beginners and often misleading. The truth is:

- Markets move sideways about **70% of the time**.
- They trend strongly only about **30% of the time**.

This means in most cases, you won't be able to make more than **1x or 2x** before the market turns back. Chasing bigger profits usually ends in frustration and losses.

We've now covered the proven methods to make money online. At this point, you might be wondering why I haven't talked about becoming an Amazon vendor. After all, it's one of the most commonly mentioned opportunities out there. The reason is simple: this book is about the methods I have personally tried and made money with. And yes, I have tried Amazon. In fact, I even attended a $900 training course on it.

But here's what I quickly realized—unless you are the *sole supplier* of a strong, unique, and in-demand product, your chances of making a real profit on Amazon are slim. The marketplace is saturated with thousands of sellers all competing to resell the same products, often at cutthroat prices. Most people source their products from platforms like Alibaba, buy in bulk, and then list them on Amazon, thinking they've struck gold. What they don't see are the hidden costs, the overwhelming competition, and the razor-thin margins.

That $900 course I attended was just the tip of the iceberg. It was designed to funnel eager beginners into another "advanced" course priced at $20,000. Behind it all was a so-called self-made millionaire in Canada, who built an empire not from Amazon sales, but from selling dreams to hopeful entrepreneurs. Sadly, many who enrolled in that $20,000 course ended up losing far more. Some invested heavily, buying large shipments from Alibaba, sending them to Amazon warehouses, and paying hefty storage fees. And yet—many of their products never sold. Some people lost not just the $20,000 course fee, but an additional $40,000 or more in unsold inventory.

The lesson is clear: unless you control a truly unique product that people want and can't easily find elsewhere, selling on Amazon will likely drain your money instead of making it. Don't fall for the glossy promises of scam courses that guarantee riches by "simply reselling" what others are already selling. Real success comes from proven paths, smart strategy, and consistency—not shortcuts sold in expensive packages.

What If None of These Six Methods Work for You — or They're Not Your Bread and Butter?

I explained how to make money through the **six main approaches** outlined in this chapter — so you can choose the one(s) that suit you best and hopefully start earning — the truth is, **not everyone will succeed with these methods.**

For example, I don't necessarily expect an **80-year-old grandmother** to start a professional website or launch a YouTube channel (though I'm absolutely certain she *could* if she really wanted to).

But here's the point:

Even for people who feel they don't have the time, skills, or energy to pursue these traditional methods, there is still a way to start making money online and move toward financial freedom — or at least take the first meaningful steps on that journey.

How LuckScout.com Makes It Possible

To help those who feel overwhelmed or unprepared for the usual paths, I created **LuckScout.com** — a platform designed to help **everyone** make money online, **for free and without any risk.**

Through **"healthy online activities,"** anyone — and I mean anyone — can start earning, regardless of age, background, or technical skill.

If this approach interests you, simply:

1. Visit LuckScout.com
2. Watch the video on the homepage
3. Sign up for a free account
4. Wait for my team to send you simple step-by-step instructions to start working.

The Sky Is the Limit

As I've said earlier, when it comes to making money online, **the sky is truly the limit.**

- Whether you're a teenager with big dreams or an **80-year-old grandma**, it is still possible to start, learn, and grow — because the online world offers limitless opportunities.
- **LuckScout.com** has made this dream possible for everyone.

There are detailed **clarifications and explanations** about this on the **LuckScout.com** website, so I encourage you to visit and review the information available there.

Closing Thoughts: Turning Online Efforts into Financial Freedom

As you've seen in this chapter, the internet offers countless doors to opportunity — from simple side hustles to full-fledged businesses. Whether it's writing, design, photography, trading, or any other method, what matters most is not just the money you can make, but the consistency, patience, and discipline you bring to the process. Each click, each upload, each trade, each effort plants seeds for future growth. The key is to start, keep going, and let time multiply your results.

Remember: every successful online income stream, no matter how small at the beginning, can grow into something powerful when combined with persistence and a long-term vision. With this foundation, you are now ready to move forward into the next stage of building financial freedom.

Looking Ahead: From Skills to Strategy

You've now explored several powerful ways to make money online — from creative arts like photography, to technical approaches like trading. Each of these methods shows you that financial freedom is not about luck, but about learning, practicing, and applying what works. But online income alone isn't enough. In the next chapter, we'll step beyond individual methods and start looking at the **bigger picture of wealth-building**: how to combine active income with passive strategies, how to protect and grow what you earn, and how to build a system that steadily moves you closer to true financial freedom.

Get ready — Chapter 4 will open a new door in your journey.

Chapter 4
Turning Earnings into Freedom

It's a good time to recall one of Warren Buffett's most remarkable quotes: *"If you don't find a way to make money while you sleep, you will work until you die."*

So far, you've learned several effective ways to make money online. But even if you start earning thousands of dollars through one or more of those methods, your financial freedom journey hasn't truly begun yet. As I explained back in Chapter 2, financial freedom is not about how much money you make — it's about how much **passive income** you create. That means you must take the active income you earn (from your online business or any other business) and force it to generate money for you without your direct involvement, even while you sleep. That's exactly what Buffett was pointing to.

Making money online is exciting. Each sale, each trade, each client payment feels like proof that your effort is paying off. But if you stop there, you'll always be working for money, stuck in the cycle of earning and spending. The real breakthrough comes when you learn to take a portion of those earnings and transform them into something greater: **passive income.** This is where money begins to work for you. No matter how small your income is today, consistently channeling even a fraction of it into smart investments creates a snowball effect that grows larger year after year. In this chapter, we'll uncover how to make that shift — how to stop relying only on active income and start building true financial freedom.

Why Passive Income Is the Real Goal

Active income — the money you earn from working, whether it's running a website, uploading videos, freelancing, or trading — is powerful. It pays the bills, supports your family, and gives you choices. But active income has one unavoidable limitation: it depends on *you*. If you stop working, the income stops too.

That's why passive income is the ultimate goal. Passive income is money that flows to you regularly with little or no daily effort. It keeps coming in whether you're working, traveling, or sleeping. It's the bridge between "making a living" and **achieving financial freedom.**

Think about it this way: if all your income is active, you are always "renting out" your time, energy, and skills. You may earn well, but you'll never truly be free because your income is chained to your activity. Passive income breaks that chain. It allows you to buy back your time and focus on what truly matters — whether that's your family, your health, your passions, or scaling your wealth even further.

Here's the key mindset shift:

- **Active income is temporary.** It only exists while you're working.
- **Passive income is permanent.** It continues regardless of your work.

This doesn't mean active income is bad — in fact, it's essential. Active income is the **fuel** that powers passive income. Without earning actively, you won't have the surplus to invest. But the moment you start forcing a portion of that active income to generate passive income, you've entered the path to financial freedom.

Imagine making $3,000 per month from your job or online business. If you commit to directing just 20% ($600) into smart investments every month, in a few years you'll have an income stream that can cover your essentials without you lifting a finger. And once your passive income exceeds your living expenses, you are free — free from financial stress, free from depending on a boss or client, free to live life on your terms.

This is why passive income is the real goal. Without it, money is always your master. With it, money becomes your servant.

The Golden Rule — Pay Yourself First

The single most important principle of building wealth is simple: **pay yourself first.**

Most people do the opposite. They earn money, pay bills, buy what they want, and then save "whatever is left." The problem is, there's rarely anything left. Lifestyle expands to match income, and saving becomes an afterthought. That's why so many people stay stuck in the cycle of working hard but never building true wealth.

To escape this trap, you must reverse the order:

1. **Every time you earn, set aside a fixed percentage for your future.**
2. **Only then** spend the rest on living expenses and wants.

This "forced discipline" is how you ensure your active income begins feeding your passive income. It's not optional — it's automatic.

How Much Should You Save?

- If you're just starting, commit to at least **10% of your income.**
- If possible, push that number higher: **20–30%** is ideal.
- Even if you start small, what matters is consistency — not the size of the first deposit.

Imagine you earn $2,000 per month. Paying yourself first at 20% means moving $400 into your "freedom account" every month before spending a single dollar on bills, food, or entertainment. Over a year, that's $4,800. Invested wisely, it won't just sit there — it will start multiplying.

The Mental Shift

When you pay yourself first, something powerful happens: you stop seeing savings and investments as optional. They become your "first bill" — non-negotiable, like rent or electricity. You train your brain to live on what's left, and surprisingly, you'll adapt quickly.

This habit doesn't just build money. It builds discipline. And discipline is what transforms income into freedom.

Generate Sources of Passive Income

Now that you understand the importance of passive income in achieving financial freedom, we arrive at the million-dollar question: **How do you actually generate it?**

I've used the word *investment* several times throughout this book, but what exactly does that mean in practice? Can you just put money into anything labeled as an "investment" and expect it to produce passive income for you? Absolutely not. Many so-called investments are nothing more than traps designed to drain your hard-earned money.

In this chapter, I'm going to explain the **best and safest ways** I know to generate true passive income. As always, I will only share methods that I've personally studied, tested, or implemented over the past decades — lessons I've learned from real mentors and real experience. These aren't just "lists of options" you can find on Google. This is about what *actually works*, if you follow it with discipline.

But before we dive into specific methods, there are some timeless principles you must keep in mind. They are non-negotiable. Forget them, and not only will you fail to create passive income — you may lose everything you've worked so hard to earn.

1. Never Rush Into an Investment

Patience is one of the most powerful tools you have as an investor. One of my golden rules is this: **never rush into an investment.**

Whenever you hear about an opportunity — whether from a friend who's excited, a news headline that looks promising, or a pitch that feels almost irresistible — your natural reaction is to want to jump in right away. That feeling of urgency isn't wisdom; it's dopamine. It's excitement tricking your mind into believing you've found something special.

But here's the truth: if an opportunity is truly good, it will still be there tomorrow. Or next week. Or even next month. That's why I always impose what I call a **cooling period** — a waiting time of at least **10 days to one month** before making any decision. During this period, you research, you analyze, you think, you consult with others, and you let your initial emotions calm down. By the end of the cooling period, the excitement fades and clarity replaces it. Many times you'll realize that what looked like a "can't-miss opportunity" was just hype.

And here's another important point: if someone tells you that you must "act now" or that "tomorrow will be too late," walk away immediately. Real investments don't pressure you. Only scams and risky schemes do.

I've learned this lesson the hard way. Every time I rushed and jumped into an investment out of excitement, I regretted it. But every time I waited, cooled down, and acted with wisdom, I either avoided a trap or made a far better decision.

So, remember this rule for life: **never rush to invest.** Let time and patience be your allies, not urgency and emotion.

2. Never Risk Too Much in a Single Investment

Another golden rule is simple but vital: **never risk too much money in any one investment, no matter how promising it looks.**

It doesn't matter if an asset has a stellar track record, glowing reviews, or years of strong performance. You've heard the phrase before: *"past performance is not a guarantee of future success."* It may sound cliché, but it's the truth. Markets are shaped by unpredictable forces — crises, pandemics, wars, policy shifts — and even the strongest investments can stumble when conditions change.

That's why you must always start small. Test the waters with a modest amount, then add more gradually over time as your confidence grows and conditions prove stable. If you invest too much too quickly, you set yourself up for panic when markets inevitably dip or crash. But if you've invested wisely and conservatively, downturns don't rattle you. Instead, you see them as opportunities. When prices fall, you calmly wait for the right moment to buy a little more.

Here's the reality: **all markets crash.** It's not a matter of *if* but *when.* The people who risked too much will lose their shirts during those crashes. But the disciplined investor who risked little, kept cash ready, and stayed patient will view every crash as a fresh chance to build wealth.

Always remind yourself: you don't invest to get rich quick. That mindset belongs to gamblers, not investors. You invest to become financially free in the long term. And that freedom only comes to those who manage risk with wisdom and humility.

3. Never Hand Over Your Money to Others

On your journey to financial freedom, you'll meet people who notice that you've been saving money and are serious about building wealth. To them, this looks like an opportunity. They will approach you with offers, schemes, or "can't-miss" investments, promising tempting profits if you just let them manage your money.

Here's the truth: the moment you hand over your money to someone else, you should consider it gone. **Never surrender control of your savings or investments.** Not only that — never reveal the details of your financial situation, your savings, or your plans to anyone. The less people know, the safer you are.

I've seen too many heartbreaking examples. People who trusted friends, relatives, or business contacts ended up losing everything — their savings, their homes, even their dignity. Some of them became homeless because they trusted the wrong person. And the saddest part? Many of these "opportunities" came from people they thought they could trust — a brother, a father-in-law, or a close friend.

It doesn't matter who it is. If someone asks for your money to "invest for you," your answer must always be **NO.** Learn to say no, firmly and without guilt. If you can't, you will never achieve your financial goals — especially financial freedom.

Remember: your money, your responsibility. Keep it that way.

4. Never Manage Other People's Money

The opposite danger is also true. As you begin doing well, people will notice. Some will approach you and ask you to invest their money for them. It might feel flattering at first, as if they trust your judgment. But don't make this mistake. The moment you accept someone else's money, you are planting the seeds of disaster — both financial and personal.

Here's why:

- **Legal risk:** Managing money for others without the proper licenses is illegal in most countries. You could face serious penalties or even jail time.
- **Relationship risk:** The fastest way to ruin friendships or family ties is to lose someone else's money. Even if the loss wasn't your fault, they will blame you.
- **Reputation risk:** The moment returns don't meet their expectations, people are quick to call you a scammer, a crook, or worse.

I've seen this play out too many times. It never ends well. Even if the request comes from your closest relative — a brother, an in-law, a lifelong friend — your answer must be a firm and respectful **NO**.

Learn to say no. Protect yourself, your relationships, and your future. Your financial freedom journey is yours alone. Do not entangle it with managing other people's money. And while we are here, let me add: **avoid partnerships as well.** Partnerships often seem like a shortcut to success, but more often they end in conflict, mistrust, and failure.

If you want to stay safe, stay independent. Your money, your choices, your responsibility.

5. Be Humble and Don't Show Off

Another timeless rule on the journey to financial freedom is humility. **Never show off your financial success.**

When things start going well, the temptation is strong to let others know — to buy flashy cars, wear expensive clothes, or drop hints about your growing wealth. But showing off only creates problems. It attracts envy, unnecessary attention, and sometimes even danger. It also puts pressure on you to keep performing for an audience instead of quietly building your freedom.

The wisest approach is to keep your business and your financial progress a secret. Live simply. Behave as if you're still striving, even when you're thriving. One of my favorite sayings is: *"Act like you need a loaf of bread, even when you own the whole bakery."*

Staying humble protects you. It keeps you safe from opportunists, keeps your ego in check, and allows you to focus on the real mission — building long-term financial freedom for yourself and your loved ones.

6. Never Invest in What You Don't Understand

This is one of the most important rules you'll ever learn in your financial freedom journey: **never put money into something you don't fully understand.**

In this book, I will share the investment methods I believe are the best — based on decades of my own learning, experience, and practice. These are the strategies that have worked for me and that I trust will work for you if you approach them with patience and discipline. But beyond what I explain here, you will constantly encounter other opportunities. The world is overflowing with "next big things," and every day someone will try to convince you that their idea, coin, fund, or scheme is the one you shouldn't miss.

Here's the truth: you don't need to chase everything. And you must not invest in anything that feels complicated, unclear, or beyond your grasp. If you don't understand how an investment generates returns, how its risks are managed, and what could go wrong — then you don't invest. Period.

I've seen countless people throw money into opportunities they didn't really understand, just because someone explained it with excitement or promised high returns. Most of them lost their money. Not because the opportunity was necessarily bad, but because they didn't understand it well enough to manage the risks.

Financial freedom doesn't come from chasing every shiny new opportunity. It comes from focusing on a few solid, proven investments you understand deeply, and committing to them over time. Remember: **an investment you don't understand is not an investment — it's a gamble.**

Now let's move on to the investment opportunities themselves and explore which ones work best — along with their pros and cons. I'll start with the harder, more complex options and work my way toward the simpler, more beginner-friendly ones that are also my personal favorites. As you go through this list, you'll notice another crucial principle in action: **diversification.**

Diversification simply means not putting all your eggs in one basket. Instead of risking all your capital in a single investment, you spread it across several different opportunities, each with a small portion of your money. This strategy protects you from major losses and increases your chances of consistent, long-term success. It's the smartest way to build wealth safely — step by step, with wisdom and balance.

1. Real Estate

Real estate is often seen as one of the best long-term investments. But let me be honest with you — it can also be one of the hardest. It usually requires significant time to raise funds, find the right property, and manage it properly. That said, if you do it wisely, real estate can become one of the most profitable and stable ways to generate passive income. That's why I start here.

Now, you may already know a lot about real estate investing and feel tempted to skip this part. Don't. Because the way I approach real estate as a tool for financial freedom is very different from what most people believe.

First, let's clear up a common misconception: **the house you live in is not really an investment.** Yes, its value may rise over time, but it does not produce any income. In fact, it costs you money — property taxes, repairs, insurance, electricity, and other expenses. While your house is technically an *asset* (because it has value and can appreciate), in practice it behaves more like a *liability* since it takes money out of your pocket every month. You only unlock its value by selling it, which also means losing your home.

This brings us to an important distinction: **assets vs. liabilities.**

- **Liabilities** are things that cost you money — your home, your car, your furniture, your jewelry.
- **Assets** are things that not only hold value but also *generate income.*

A true real estate investment, unlike your personal home, falls into the second category. It appreciates in value over time *and* produces regular income, such as rental payments. That's the kind of real estate that can support your journey toward financial freedom.

Now let's make this as simple as possible — but not simpler, as Einstein famously said. Earlier in this book, I mentioned that whenever I face a challenge, I start by simplifying it. The same approach applies to real estate investing.

Whether you already own a home or not, your real estate investment journey is completely separate. Here's the process in simple steps:

1. **Save for Your Down Payment**
   As I explained at the beginning of this chapter, you must save a reasonable portion of your active income until you can afford the down payment on a property. Aim for at least **30% down.** Yes, some people rush in with 5–10% down payments, but that's a huge mistake. Why? Because their mortgage payments become too high, eating up any profit for years. In many countries, putting less than 30% down also requires mortgage insurance — yet another unnecessary expense.

2. **Choose the Right Property**
   Once you have your down payment, buy an apartment in a strong, active real estate market and rent it out. Don't try to do this blindly. Work with an experienced real estate agent who knows the area well, and be upfront about your goal: you want a property that will rent quickly and consistently. Location and rental demand matter more than fancy features.

3. **Start Small, Grow Gradually**
   You don't need luxury apartments in high-end buildings. Those are harder to rent because their rents are too high. Instead, start small — modest apartments in accessible neighborhoods. They're easier to rent out and will give you stable cash flow.

4. **Build Passive Income and Equity Together**
   Your tenants' rent will cover your mortgage payments, while the property itself appreciates in value over time. That's two benefits at once: steady passive income and long-term growth in wealth.

5. **Repeat the Process**
   Don't stop after one property. Keep saving, keep reinvesting, and buy more apartments over time. Gradually, you'll reach the point where the rental income from your properties not only covers your living expenses but also leaves you with extra money to expand further. This is the moment when real estate becomes more than an investment — it becomes the engine of your financial freedom.

That's the beauty of real estate: it's not complicated when broken down into steps, and it rewards patience and discipline.

Everything we do in this world carries some level of risk. Even drinking water, crossing the street, or leaving home involves risk. Real estate investing is no different. It has both **advantages** that can build your wealth and **disadvantages** that you must be prepared to handle. Understanding both sides is essential if you want to approach real estate with wisdom instead of emotion.

The Pros of Real Estate Investing

1. **Steady Passive Income**
   Rental properties can provide consistent monthly cash flow. Even one property can cover part of your living expenses, and multiple properties can fully support your lifestyle.

2. **Appreciation Over Time**
   Real estate typically increases in value over the long term. While prices may fluctuate in the short run, history shows that

property values trend upward, especially in strong markets.

3. **Leverage**
   Real estate allows you to use other people's money (the bank's mortgage) to build wealth. With a down payment, you control a much larger asset than you could buy outright.

4. **Inflation Protection**
   Rents usually rise with inflation, which means your income increases while your mortgage payment (if it's fixed) stays the same. Over time, this widens your profit margin.

5. **Multiple Income Streams**
   A single property can generate both rental income (short-term cash flow) and appreciation (long-term profit).

6. **Path to Financial Freedom**
   Once you own several properties, the rental income can exceed your expenses, allowing you to live fully off passive income.

The Cons of Real Estate Investing

1. **High Upfront Costs**
   Saving for a 30% down payment takes time and discipline. Real estate isn't a "quick start" investment.

2. **Maintenance and Repairs**
   Properties need ongoing attention — fixing leaks, replacing appliances, dealing with tenant issues. This requires time, money, or hiring a property manager.

3. **Vacancies**
   There will be times when your property sits empty. No tenants means no rental income, but your mortgage and other expenses still need to be paid.

4. **Market Fluctuations**
   Real estate markets rise and fall. A downturn can lower property values temporarily and put pressure on landlords.

5. **Liquidity**
   Unlike stocks, you can't sell part of your property quickly to raise cash. Real estate is a long-term commitment.

6. **Responsibility**
   Being a landlord means responsibility for tenants, legal requirements, and financial management. Not everyone is ready for this role.

Remember, real estate is not about getting rich quick. It's about achieving financial freedom over the long term. Those who chase quick wealth in real estate are usually the ones who take excessive risks — and they are also the ones most likely to lose everything through foreclosure.

As I've already told you, all markets crash at some point. Real estate is no exception. But here's the difference: if you start small, save properly and put down at least 30%, you give yourself the ability to hold on through downturns. When the market eventually recovers, your property will still be there, and your wealth will continue to grow.

On the other hand, those who rush in with tiny down payments and massive mortgages often can't survive the crash. Their monthly payments overwhelm them, and when the market drops, they're forced to default.

This, perhaps, is the biggest secret of real estate investing: **go slow, be wise, and build surely.** The patient investor wins, while the reckless one loses.

Does This Really Work?

The best way to answer that question is with a real story. Let me share with you the remarkable journey of a woman who taught me a valuable lesson — even after decades of business experience, when I thought I had already learned it all.

This story reminded me of something crucial: no matter how knowledgeable or experienced we think we are, we should always stay open to learning. Wisdom can come from unexpected places, and sometimes the simplest lessons are the most powerful.

So here's her story...

Many people believe that unless they are born wealthy or earn a high salary, financial freedom is impossible. But that's simply not true. I got to know a cleaning lady just recently who proved this in the most remarkable way. She didn't have a high-paying job or a glamorous life. She worked long hours, saved carefully, invested wisely—and she ended up a millionaire.

Hopefully, one day I will record a full and detailed interview with her—if she agrees—and share it with you, because she has tremendously inspired me and had a strong impact on the way I think about money and investment, even though I thought I knew everything I needed to know. In the meantime, let me share her story with you, without names or unnecessary drama—just pure facts and numbers.

This lady earned modest wages throughout her life. Yet, every year, she managed to save about $3,000. As time went on and her situation improved slightly, she even managed to save $5,000 a year—combining her job earnings with the small cash flow from her investments.

She focused on **buying small apartments**—not in expensive cities, but in affordable neighborhoods where property prices were reasonable and rental demand was steady.

Here's roughly how her journey unfolded:

Years 1–5: Saved $3,000–$5,000 per year. After 5 years, she had around $20,000 saved. Bought her first small apartment with a mortgage, using the $20,000 as a down payment.

Years 5–10: The rental income covered the mortgage payments and provided a little extra cash flow. She kept saving $3,000 to $5,000 a year from her job and the rental cash flow. Property values started rising. To buy her second property, she now needed a larger down payment. After 5 more years, she had saved around $30,000.

Year 10: Bought her second apartment, again using a mortgage and $30,000 as a down payment.

Years 10–20: Now she had two apartments generating rental income. She continued saving and using the rental income to pay off her mortgages faster. By the end of 20 years, both properties were almost or completely paid off, and each had appreciated significantly.

Years 20–30: She bought a third and even a fourth apartment, using her savings and rental income from the first two properties. Rents had increased over time, boosting her monthly income even more.

Year 30+: She owned four fully paid-off apartments, each generating solid and growing rental income. The value of her real estate portfolio had soared after decades of steady appreciation.

Here's a rough but realistic estimate:

- Initial property purchase price (first apartment): **around $100,000**
- Property price by second purchase: **around $130,000–$150,000**
- Property price by third and fourth purchases: **around $180,000–$220,000**
- Average appreciation: **3%–4% per year**

After 30–35 years:

- Each apartment could now be worth **$300,000–$400,000.**
- Owning **four** apartments worth around **$350,000** each means a portfolio value of **$1.4 million.**
- Add years of rental income (even modestly averaging $15,000–$25,000 per year per property), and her total net worth easily surpasses **$2 million.**

She kept doing this patiently, and it is several years that she is a millionaire with a net worth of **over $2 million**. And guess what?

Do you think how old she is? She is currently 60 years old. She started in her 20s—and by the age of 50–55, when most people are nearing retirement age and feeling stressed because they have little to no savings, she was already fully financially free.

Many people today, even those who worked hard all their lives, are facing retirement with empty bank accounts. Some who tried to invest in risky markets have lost a big portion of their savings during the recent market crashes.

But this cleaning lady followed a simple and consistent strategy—and won.

Is Financial Freedom Her Only Achievement? No! She has developed the strong character of a consistent and disciplined investor—something you rarely see even among highly educated people or those in high positions, many of whom still live paycheck to paycheck and suffer from a lack of discipline, consistency, and emotional control. When you commit yourself seriously to achieving financial freedom, financial freedom won't be the only thing you accomplish.

Maybe you're thinking, "Well, I'm not in my 20s anymore."

That's okay. Even if you start now, you can still achieve half or more of what she has achieved by 60—and that's still life-changing. Even if you are 60 now, if you do what that lady did, you can still build a cash flow by 70. And what if you live to 95 or even longer? You could have at least 25 to 35 years ahead of you.

We are now done with the real estate investment section. I hope you've enjoyed it and, more importantly, that you've seen how powerful it can be when approached with patience and discipline. But this is only the beginning of your investment journey.

The next part may be even more interesting for you — it's about **gold**, one of humanity's oldest and most trusted stores of value. And beyond gold, the most exciting and important investment strategies are still waiting for you. So let's keep going.

2. Gold

Gold is one of the oldest and most trusted forms of wealth in human history. For over **5,000 years**, civilizations across every continent have valued gold as a universal form of money, trade, and security. From the ancient Egyptians who buried it with their kings, to the Roman Empire that minted it into coins, to the gold standards that backed modern currencies until just a century ago — gold has always been seen as *real money*.

What makes gold special is its **scarcity.** Unlike paper currencies that governments can print at will, the total amount of gold on Earth is fixed. Every ounce that exists has either been mined or is still deep underground, waiting to be discovered. This limited supply is one of the reasons gold has preserved its value for thousands of years.

Another unique feature of gold is its resilience. Empires rise and fall, currencies come and go, economies crash and recover — yet gold has always remained valuable. In fact, measured over long periods, the price of gold has consistently moved upward. A hundred years ago, one ounce of gold could buy you a fine suit. Today, one ounce of gold can still buy you a fine suit — and in most cases, a much better one.

Gold is not just a shiny metal. It is a **tangible store of wealth** that has stood the test of time. And in today's uncertain world — with inflation, debt, and global crises always around the corner — gold remains one of the safest and most reliable ways to protect and grow your money.

In spite of all this, an important question remains: **Can gold really help you advance on your financial freedom journey?**

Well... as I've mentioned many times in this book, the key to financial freedom is to force your money to generate **passive income** for you. Real estate does this beautifully because you can rent out properties and collect steady rental payments. Gold, however, is different. Gold does not generate passive income. You can only buy it, hold it, and wait for its value to rise over time.

So why is gold still worth considering? Because it's an excellent way to **preserve the value of your money.** Inflation steadily eats away at your purchasing power. A $100 bill you save today will still be $100 ten years from now, but will it buy you the same things? Definitely not. Prices rise nonstop, fueled by inflation and by central banks printing unbacked fiat currency.

Gold protects you from this erosion. If you take that same $100 today and buy gold, then hold it for ten years, chances are high that it will be worth much more. When you sell it later, you'll be able to buy the same things — and often more — than you could buy with $100 today.

That's the role of gold: it's not about creating income, but about **preserving wealth.** It acts like a shield, protecting your hard work and savings from being silently devalued over time.

Please note that here I am talking specifically about **pure physical gold — 24 karat gold.** Forget about jewelry, mixed karats, or any other forms you see in the market. And I am also not talking about buying shares of gold mining companies. Those companies can lose value even while the price of gold itself is rising. If your goal is to **lock in the value of your money**, the only way is to buy and hold pure gold. And you must be prepared to hold it for decades.

But let's also be clear about the **cons.**

1. **Storage and Safety Risks**
   Keeping physical gold is not easy. If you store it at home, you face the risk of theft. Worse, if others know you have gold, it can even become life-threatening. The safer option is to store it in a bank's safety deposit box, but this comes with a cost. In short, gold is not free to keep safe.

2. **Liquidity Challenges**
   Even after many years, when the value of your gold has increased significantly, you still need to sell it to realize your profit. That can sometimes be tricky. Finding a buyer is not always easy, and often, buyers (especially jewelers or dealers) will offer you less than the official market price. This means you may not get the full value you expect.

3. **No Cash Flow**
   Unlike real estate, gold does not generate passive income while

you hold it. It just sits there, holding value until you decide to sell.

Despite these challenges, gold remains a powerful tool for **wealth preservation.** If you keep it long enough, it almost always protects you from inflation and economic crises. But you must understand both the benefits and the limitations before committing to it.

In general, I am not a fan of investing in gold, mainly because financial freedom requires building **passive income** — and gold doesn't generate any. I included gold here because I couldn't ignore it as a respected store of value and a hedge against inflation. It has its place, but it's not the vehicle that will carry you all the way to financial freedom.

As I mentioned at the beginning of this chapter, I'm starting with the harder or less effective investment methods before moving into the ones I truly recommend — the ones that generate steady passive income. So far, you've learned that real estate is powerful but requires significant capital and effort. Gold is stable but doesn't create income.

Now, let's move on to the next opportunities — ones that may be even more practical and accessible for building long-term wealth, and especially powerful when it comes to generating **passive income.**

3. Stocks

When it comes to stocks, I want you to pause and set aside everything you think you already know. Don't say to yourself, *"I've heard all this before"* and skip ahead. Yes, you may have heard about stocks, maybe even bought or traded some in the past. But the way I approach stocks in the context of financial freedom is different.

Our goal, as always, is to **generate passive income** while also growing our capital over time.

Sure, you can buy and hold some stocks and hope their prices go up. If they do, you sell them later and collect a profit. But think about it: isn't this exactly what you would do with gold? That's why I told you earlier that I'm not a big fan of gold — because it doesn't generate passive income. Most stocks fall into the same category. You buy, you hold, and if they rise, you sell. That's not true financial freedom.

Here's where stocks differ from gold: stocks are not physical, so you don't have to worry about storing them, keeping them safe, or paying fees to protect them. They exist digitally, which makes them much easier to own. But that still doesn't make ordinary stocks the best vehicle for financial freedom.

What I want to focus on here is something different: **dividend stocks.** These are shares of companies that pay you a portion of their profits — your share — simply for owning them. Unlike ordinary stocks where you only profit when you sell, dividend stocks pay you regularly, month after month or quarter after quarter, while you continue to hold them. This transforms stocks from a gamble on price increases into a true source of passive income.

What Are Dividend Stocks and Why Do They Matter?

Most companies reinvest their profits back into growth, expansion, or debt repayment. But some of the strongest, most stable companies share a portion of their profits directly with their shareholders. These are called **dividends.**

When you own a dividend stock, you're not just waiting for the price to go up so you can sell — you're actually **getting paid to hold it.** Think of it like owning a small piece of a business that mails you a "thank-you check" every month or every quarter. The company does the hard work of running the business, and you, as an investor, share in the profits.

This is where dividend stocks stand apart from ordinary stocks and even from gold:

- **Gold preserves wealth** but generates no income.
- **Non-dividend stocks grow wealth** only if you sell them later.
- **Dividend stocks grow wealth AND generate income** while you hold them.

That's why dividend stocks can be such a powerful tool for financial freedom. They can:

1. **Create reliable passive income** — regular cash payments you can reinvest or use to cover expenses.
2. **Grow in value over time** — because the stock price itself can still rise, giving you the best of both worlds.
3. **Reinvest automatically** — many brokers let you reinvest dividends back into buying more shares, compounding your wealth faster.

The best part? Once you've built a portfolio of strong dividend-paying companies, those payments keep coming whether you work or not. That's passive income in action.

How to Start Investing in Dividend Stocks

1. Choose a Reliable Broker

To buy dividend stocks, you first need a brokerage account. Today, many online brokers make this easy, with user-friendly apps and websites. Look for one that:

- Has low or zero commissions on stock trades.
- Allows dividend reinvestment (often called a *DRIP: Dividend Reinvestment Plan*).
- Provides research tools and a simple dashboard.
  Examples include Fidelity, Charles Schwab, Interactive Brokers, TD Ameritrade, or even beginner-friendly platforms like Robinhood or Webull (though I recommend brokers with a longer history and stronger customer support).

2. Understand Dividend Yield

Dividend yield is the percentage of a company's stock price that it pays back to shareholders as dividends each year. For example, if a stock costs $100 and pays $4 annually in dividends, its yield is 4%.

- **Too high** a yield (like 12% or more) can be a red flag — it might mean the company is struggling and trying to attract investors.
- **Too low** (like under 1%) may not be worth your time.
- The sweet spot is usually **2–6%**, depending on your goals and risk tolerance.

3. Look for Dividend Aristocrats

A great starting point is with companies known as **Dividend Aristocrats** — businesses that have increased their dividends every single year for at least 25 years. These are often strong, stable companies like Johnson & Johnson, Coca-Cola, or Procter & Gamble. They may not have flashy returns, but they are reliable, which is exactly what you want for financial freedom.

4. Diversify Your Dividend Portfolio

Don't put all your money into one company. Build a basket of dividend-paying stocks across different industries — for example, consumer goods, healthcare, utilities, and technology. This spreads your risk and makes your income stream more stable.

5. Reinvest Dividends

In the beginning, don't cash out your dividends. Reinvest them automatically to buy more shares. This creates a compounding effect where your income grows faster over time — the snowball effect that makes dividend investing so powerful.

6. Be Patient

Dividend investing is not a "get rich quick" strategy. It's slow, steady, and reliable. Think in terms of **years and decades, not weeks.** Over time, the combination of reinvested dividends and stock appreciation can turn even small investments into large streams of passive income.

A Real-World Example of Dividend Growth

Let's imagine you start with **$1,000** invested in dividend stocks today. On average, good dividend stocks yield around **4% per year**. That means your $1,000 would pay you **$40 in dividends** in the first year.

Now, here's where the magic of compounding comes in: instead of spending that $40, you reinvest it to buy more shares. Next year, you don't just earn dividends on your original $1,000 — you also earn on the extra $40.

And let's say you keep adding **$1,000 every year** into your dividend portfolio, consistently, and reinvest every dividend you receive. Here's how the numbers can play out (assuming an average 4% dividend yield and modest 5% stock price growth per year):

- **After 10 years**:
  Your total contributions = $10,000
  Portfolio value (with growth + reinvested dividends) ≈ **$15,600**
  Annual dividend income ≈ **$625 per year** — almost like getting a free paycheck every month.

- **After 20 years**:
  Your total contributions = $20,000
  Portfolio value ≈ **$53,000**
  Annual dividend income ≈ **$2,100 per year** — enough to cover bills or small lifestyle expenses, without touching your invested capital.

- **After 30 years**:
  Your total contributions = $30,000
  Portfolio value ≈ **$133,000**
  Annual dividend income ≈ **$5,300 per year** — now you're generating real passive income, while your portfolio keeps growing.

The numbers may look simple, but this is the **snowball effect** in action. With consistency, patience, and reinvestment, small amounts grow into life-changing income streams. The earlier you start and the longer you stay consistent, the bigger the snowball becomes.

This is why dividend stocks are such a powerful part of the financial freedom journey. They turn your active income into an asset that pays you again and again — whether you work or not.

The Pros of Dividend Investing

1. **Passive Income Stream**
    Dividend stocks pay you regularly, often quarterly, whether you work or not. This creates a steady income stream that can cover expenses or be reinvested for faster growth.

2. **Compounding Power**
    Reinvesting dividends allows your money to grow on top of itself. Over time, this snowball effect can turn small, consistent contributions into substantial wealth.

3. **Potential for Capital Gains**
    Unlike bonds or fixed savings, dividend stocks can also increase in price. This means you benefit from both income (dividends) and growth (rising stock prices).

4. **Flexibility**
    You decide whether to cash out dividends for income or reinvest them. This makes dividend investing adaptable to different stages of your financial journey — growth now, income later.

5. **Proven Companies**
    Many dividend-paying stocks are strong, established businesses with long track records of stability. Companies known as *Dividend Aristocrats* (those that have raised dividends for 25+ years in a row) are often among the most reliable investments in the world.

The Cons of Dividend Investing

1. **Lower Immediate Growth Potential**
    Companies that pay dividends often grow more slowly than high-growth companies that reinvest all profits back into expansion. This means you may not see huge short-term stock

price jumps.

2. **Taxes on Dividends**
   Depending on your country, dividends may be taxed as income. This can reduce your net returns if you are not using tax-advantaged accounts.

3. **Dividend Cuts**
   Dividends are not guaranteed. In tough times, even strong companies can reduce or suspend dividends, which lowers your income and can also drop the stock price.

4. **Requires Patience**
   Dividend investing is a long-term game. If you're looking for quick money, this strategy will disappoint you. Its true power only shows after years of reinvesting and compounding.

5. **Market Risk Still Exists**
   Stock prices fluctuate. While dividends help cushion the ups and downs, you can still lose money if you panic and sell during downturns.

Dividend investing is not a get-rich-quick path. It's a **steady, reliable strategy** that rewards consistency, patience, and discipline. If you stick with it, dividend stocks can become one of the strongest passive income streams in your financial freedom journey.

Now, I'd like to share another real story with you. Unlike the story of the cleaning lady that only those around her knew, this one went viral after it was published in the *Wall Street Journal*. It's a powerful reminder of what consistency, discipline, and long-term thinking can do.

The Janitor Who Became a Millionaire

Ronald Read was not a man anyone expected to become wealthy. He spent most of his life working as a gas station attendant, mechanic, and part-time janitor. His income was modest, and his lifestyle was even more modest. He drove an old Toyota Yaris, wore patched clothing, chopped his own firewood, and lived quietly in Vermont. To those who knew him, he seemed like an ordinary man with simple habits.

What no one realized was that Ronald had a secret. Quietly, year after year, he had been investing in dividend-paying stocks. He never chased risky companies or tried to "time the market." Instead, he focused on businesses he understood — strong, reliable companies like Johnson & Johnson, Procter & Gamble, and Wells Fargo. Every dividend he earned was reinvested, buying him more shares and slowly increasing the size of his portfolio. He did this consistently, decade after decade, without fanfare or attention.

When Ronald passed away in 2014 at the age of 92, the truth came out. His estate was worth nearly **eight million dollars**, much of it built through the power of compounding dividends. The story shocked his community — and soon after, it was featured in the *Wall Street Journal*, where it inspired millions around the world.

What made Ronald's story even more remarkable was how he chose to use his fortune. Instead of spending lavishly, he left most of it behind to support his local hospital and community library. The janitor who had once been overlooked ended up leaving a legacy that changed lives.

His life teaches us a profound lesson: you don't need a high income or a glamorous career to achieve financial freedom. What you need is consistency, patience, and the discipline to reinvest in reliable dividend-paying companies. Ronald Read's story proves that ordinary people can achieve extraordinary results if they stick to the plan and let time do the heavy lifting.

The story of Ronald Read proves something powerful: you don't need to be a Wall Street expert, a millionaire, or even have a high-paying job to build wealth. What you need is **patience, discipline, and consistency.** By living simply, investing regularly in dividend-paying companies, and letting time and compounding do their work, he turned an ordinary life into an extraordinary legacy.

That's the real beauty of dividend investing. It's not flashy, it's not fast, and it's not about gambling on risky stocks. It's about creating a steady flow of passive income that grows alongside your capital, year after year. Whether your goal is financial freedom for yourself or leaving something behind for your family or community, dividend stocks can help you get there.

Now that we've covered real estate, gold, and stocks, you're starting to see the bigger picture: not every investment is about quick profits, but each has a role to play in your financial freedom journey. In the next section, we'll move into another way of making your money work for you — one that offers a different kind of opportunity and risk — as we continue building the roadmap toward lasting wealth.

4. Index Funds

If you've ever looked at the stock market and thought, *"It's too complicated — how do I even choose the right stocks?"* then index funds might be the perfect answer for you. They are one of the **simplest and most powerful tools** available to ordinary people who want to grow wealth and generate passive income.

What Is an Index Fund?

An index fund is a type of mutual fund or exchange-traded fund (ETF) that simply follows a market index like the **S&P 500**. Instead of trying to pick winning stocks, the fund automatically buys and holds shares of all the companies in that index. That means if you buy one share of an S&P 500 index fund, you instantly own a small piece of 500 of the largest U.S. companies — Apple, Microsoft, Coca-Cola, Johnson & Johnson, and many more.

This makes index funds a powerful tool because they provide **instant diversification.** You don't need to research individual companies, worry about missing the "next big stock," or fear that one mistake will wipe you out. With an index fund, your money is spread across hundreds of businesses, reducing your risk.

Why Index Funds Work So Well

The magic of index funds lies in their **simplicity and reliability.**

- **They beat most professionals**: Study after study has shown that over the long run, most actively managed funds (where experts pick stocks) actually underperform simple index funds.

- **They're low cost**: Because they don't need expensive fund managers to make decisions, index funds charge very low fees — sometimes less than 0.05%. That means more of your money stays invested and growing.

- **They're passive**: Once you buy them, you don't need to manage them. The fund automatically adjusts as companies enter or leave the index.

Warren Buffett himself has said that if most people simply invested in a low-cost S&P 500 index fund and held it long-term, they would outperform the majority of investors and fund managers.

How Index Funds Generate Passive Income

Index funds not only grow in value over time but many also **pay dividends.** Since the companies inside the index pay dividends, those are passed on to you as the shareholder. You can choose to take those dividends as cash or reinvest them to buy more shares, compounding your returns year after year.

Example of Growth Over Time

Imagine investing **$500 a month** into an S&P 500 index fund. Over 20 years, assuming an average 8% annual return (a conservative historical average for the S&P 500), your total contributions would be $120,000. But your portfolio could grow to **over $275,000** — more than double what you put in. And that's without needing to pick a single stock or time the market.

Why I Recommend Index Funds

Unlike gold, which only protects your wealth, or individual stocks, which can be risky and unpredictable, index funds give you the best of both worlds: **growth and income.** They are simple, safe for beginners, and incredibly powerful over the long term. They are not a get-rich-quick scheme, but they are one of the strongest tools for achieving financial freedom if you stay consistent.

How to Invest in Index Funds: A Step-by-Step Guide

Step 1: Choose a Brokerage Account

To buy an index fund, you need a brokerage account. Many online brokers offer access to index funds and ETFs with **zero commissions** and **low fees.** Popular and reliable options include Fidelity, Vanguard, Charles Schwab, and TD Ameritrade. For ETFs (exchange-traded funds), almost every major broker will do. Look for:

- Low or no trading fees.
- Access to index funds like the S&P 500.
- Automatic dividend reinvestment (called DRIP: Dividend Reinvestment Plan).

Step 2: Select the Index You Want to Track

The most common choice is the **S&P 500**, because it represents 500 of the largest U.S. companies. Other popular options include:

- **Total Market Index Funds** (covering the entire U.S. stock market).
- **International Index Funds** (covering non-U.S. companies).
- **Specialized Index Funds** (like technology or healthcare sectors, though these are less diversified).

If you're new, starting with an **S&P 500 index fund** is usually the simplest and strongest choice.

Step 3: Decide How Much to Invest

Don't wait until you have a huge amount of money saved. Start small — even $100 or $500 is enough to get going. The power of index funds lies in **consistency**, not the size of your first investment.

Step 4: Set Up Automatic Contributions

The secret to building wealth with index funds is not trying to "time the market," but consistently adding money. Almost all brokers let you set up automatic monthly contributions. Decide on an amount you can comfortably invest — for example, **$200 a month** — and let the system do the work.

Step 5: Reinvest Dividends

When your index fund pays dividends, choose the option to automatically reinvest them into buying more shares. This simple habit allows your money to compound faster, accelerating your path to financial freedom.

Step 6: Hold and Be Patient

Index funds are a **long-term game.** Don't panic if the market dips — that's normal. Remember, the S&P 500 has always recovered after every crash in history. The key is to keep contributing and holding for the long term. Over years and decades, the compounding effect will surprise you.

Investing in index funds is one of the easiest, safest, and most effective ways to turn your active income into **passive wealth growth.** You don't need to pick individual stocks, study the markets every day, or gamble with risky trades. Instead, you just set up your account, invest consistently, reinvest dividends, and let time do the heavy lifting.

A Real-World Example of Index Fund Growth

Imagine you decide to invest **$500 per month** into an S&P 500 index fund. That's $6,000 per year. You keep this up consistently, year after year, without skipping. Historically, the S&P 500 has returned around **8% per year** on average (after inflation).

Here's what that could look like:

- **After 10 years**:
  You've invested $60,000 total.
  With growth, your portfolio could be worth about **$91,000**.
  That's $31,000 more than what you put in — and much of that growth came from compounding.

- **After 20 years**:
  You've invested $120,000 total.
  Your portfolio could be worth about **$274,000**.
  That's more than **double your contributions.**

- **After 30 years**:
  You've invested $180,000 total.
  Your portfolio could be worth about **$680,000**.
  That's nearly **half a million dollars of growth** created by compounding alone.

Now, imagine if you reinvest all dividends instead of taking them out — your money snowballs even faster, because every dividend buys you more shares, which then earn more dividends.

The Lesson

This example shows why index funds are so powerful for ordinary investors. You don't need to chase hot stocks, guess the next big winner, or spend your life analyzing charts. All you need is:

1. A simple index fund,
2. Consistent monthly contributions, and
3. Patience to let time do the heavy lifting.

Over years and decades, the results become life-changing. This is how many people with regular jobs and average incomes quietly build six- and seven-figure portfolios.

The Pros of Index Funds

1. Simplicity

You don't need to study the stock market every day or pick individual companies. With one index fund, you automatically own hundreds (or even thousands) of stocks, giving you instant diversification.

2. Proven Long-Term Growth

The S&P 500, for example, has averaged around 8% annual returns after inflation for nearly a century. Few investment methods can match that kind of long-term consistency.

3. Low Cost

Because index funds don't need active managers to pick stocks, their fees are extremely low — often close to zero. This means more of your money stays invested and compounding.

4. Passive Income Through Dividends

Most index funds include dividend-paying companies, so you also receive regular dividend payments in addition to long-term growth. Reinvesting those dividends makes the snowball roll even faster.

5. Hard to Beat

Even most professional money managers underperform index funds over time. That means by simply buying and holding an index fund, you can outperform the majority of "experts" — without stress.

The Cons of Index Funds

1. Market-Dependent

When the market drops, your index fund drops with it. While history shows the market always recovers, this requires patience and discipline not to sell in panic.

2. No Outperformance

Index funds match the market — they don't beat it. If you're chasing quick, above-average gains, index funds won't give you that. They're designed for stability, not gambling.

3. Requires Time

The power of index funds lies in decades, not months. If you're looking for overnight wealth, this isn't it. But if you're willing to stay consistent for years, the results are powerful.

4. Limited Control

When you buy an index fund, you buy the whole index — good companies and not-so-good ones alike. You can't choose only the businesses you like.

Index funds are not glamorous, but they are one of the most reliable, beginner-friendly, and time-tested ways to grow wealth. If you stay consistent and patient, index funds can quietly build you a six- or seven-figure portfolio while you focus on your life and career.

Index funds show us that wealth doesn't have to come from complexity. You don't need to be glued to the stock market every day, you don't need advanced strategies, and you don't need to outsmart Wall Street. All you need is a simple, steady plan: invest consistently, reinvest your dividends, and give time the chance to multiply your results. Index funds may not be flashy, but their power lies in reliability. For many ordinary people, they are the quiet path to extraordinary wealth.

We've now looked at real estate, gold, stocks, and index funds — each with their strengths and limitations. Together, they give you a deeper understanding of how to make your active income work harder for you. But there are still other opportunities worth considering, some of which may surprise you with how practical and rewarding they can be. Let's move on and explore the next one.

5. Bitcoin

I know some traditional investors — including my mentor, legend, and role model Warren Buffett — don't recommend putting any money into Bitcoin. They have their reasons. Buffett has famously said that Bitcoin isn't linked to a real, tangible business, product, or service. And that's true. Bitcoin doesn't own factories, it doesn't sell goods, and it doesn't provide a service.

But here's the reality: **things have changed.** Bitcoin has become something new in the financial world — a **wealth container.** Even if it isn't tied to a traditional business, it represents stored value that's protected by an unbreakable digital system called **blockchain.**

Now, don't worry. I'm not going to turn this into a technical lecture about how Bitcoin is mined, or how blockchain works behind the scenes. That's not the purpose of this book. This book is about practical steps — strategies that anyone, even an 80-year-old grandma, can apply. So, let's skip the heavy computer science and talk about what matters for you: **how Bitcoin can play a role in your journey toward financial freedom.**

I'll be honest with you: I am personally a fan of Bitcoin. And I'm not alone. Over the last decade, millions of investors — many of them just as skeptical as Warren Buffett — have been won over. Bitcoin has earned its place in the global financial conversation. Big institutions, hedge funds, and even governments are now holding or regulating it.

But before you rush in, you must understand this: **Bitcoin is not like real estate, or dividend stocks, or index funds.** It comes with its own rules, risks, and rewards. If you want to invest in Bitcoin, there are some extremely important things you need to know first. In this section, I'm going to reveal them step by step, so you can decide wisely whether it deserves a place in your financial freedom plan.

What Makes Bitcoin Unique as an Investment

The first thing to understand about Bitcoin is that it's not like traditional currencies or investments. It's a **new kind of asset**, built on rules that are very different from anything else in the financial world.

1. Limited Supply

Unlike paper money, which governments can print endlessly, Bitcoin has a hard cap of **21 million coins.** That's it. Once the last coin is mined, no more will ever exist. This scarcity is what gives Bitcoin its strength. While inflation eats away at the value of dollars, euros, or yen, Bitcoin's supply cannot be inflated — making it a strong hedge against money printing and currency devaluation.

2. Decentralization

Bitcoin isn't controlled by any government, bank, or corporation. It runs on a decentralized network of computers spread all over the world, all verifying transactions through blockchain technology. This means no one can shut it down, freeze it, or manipulate it the way central banks sometimes influence currencies. For many investors, this independence makes Bitcoin a safe haven in uncertain times.

3. "Digital Gold"

Because of its scarcity and independence, Bitcoin has earned the nickname **"digital gold."** Like gold, it doesn't generate cash flow or dividends. But it holds value, and over time, its price has shown an upward trend despite extreme volatility. Many investors use it as a store of wealth, similar to how people have used gold for thousands of years.

4. Global Accessibility

Anyone with an internet connection can buy, hold, and transfer Bitcoin. You don't need permission from a bank, and there are no borders. This makes it one of the first truly global assets in history, available equally to someone in New York, Nairobi, or New Delhi.

5. Volatility and Opportunity

Of course, Bitcoin comes with a warning: it's **extremely volatile.** Prices can swing 10%, 20%, even 50% in a matter of weeks. This makes it risky if you put too much of your wealth into it. But for those who allocate wisely — usually a small percentage of their portfolio —

Bitcoin can provide significant upside potential that no traditional investment can match.

6. Immediate Liquidity

One of Bitcoin's greatest advantages is how quickly it can be converted into cash. Unlike real estate, which may take months (or even years) to sell — often forcing you to lower the price just to find a buyer — or gold, which is usually bought below the market rate by dealers, Bitcoin can be sold **instantly at market price.** No waiting, no haggling. With just a few clicks, you can liquidate your holdings anytime, day or night, thanks to 24/7 global markets. This makes Bitcoin one of the most liquid assets in the world.

Why Bitcoin's Price History Matters

Bitcoin's journey since 2009 is nothing short of a financial rollercoaster. Built on innovation, scarcity, and global trust — yet marked by extreme volatility — its story offers powerful lessons.

Explosive Growth Over Time

- Since its creation, Bitcoin has demonstrated remarkable growth. Over the past 13 years, it has posted a **compound annual growth rate (CAGR) of about 102%**, meaning it doubled in value on average **every single year**.

- Over the last 5 years alone, Bitcoin's average yearly return has been approximately **155%**, dwarfing traditional assets such as gold.

  Here are some real annual returns to give perspective:

- In 2016, Bitcoin rose **123%**.
- In 2017, it soared by a staggering **1,369%** — one of its most dramatic years.
- Even in recent years, after several crashes, it bounced back with a **155% return in 2023**, and over **120% in 2024**.

Extreme Volatility and Deep Crashes

However, the road wasn't smooth — Bitcoin is infamous for dramatic crashes:

- In **2014**, it dropped **61%** from its peak.
- In **2018**, it plunged **73%**.
- In **2022**, it fell **64%**.
- When measuring peak-to-trough drops, the deepest crash occurred between late 2013 and early 2015, hitting a staggering **86% decline**.

These wild swings reflect both Bitcoin's speculative nature and its sensitivity to news, regulations, and market sentiment.

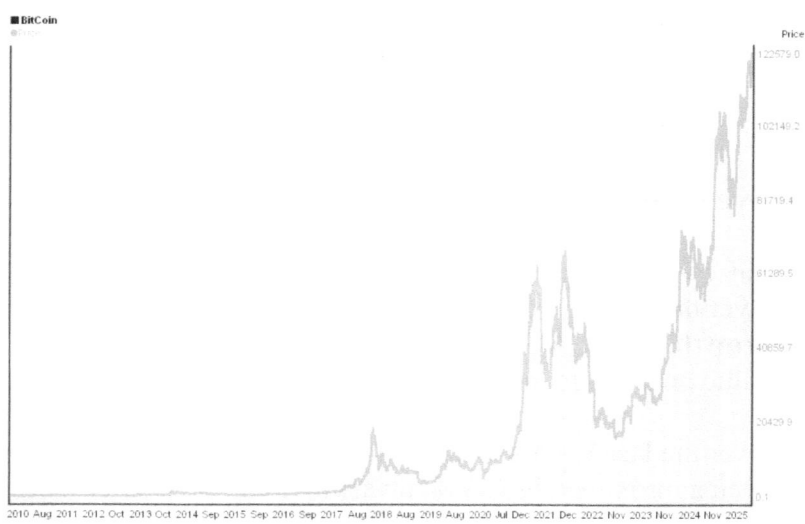

What This Means for You

Bitcoin's history is a fierce mix of excitement and caution. While it offers impressive opportunities for long-term growth — especially when held patiently — it's also a test of conviction and composure.

Use this insight wisely:

- Recognize both the upside potential and the possibility of steep, emotional downturns.
- If you decide to include Bitcoin as part of your financial plan, treat it as a high-risk, small allocation only — not the core of your portfolio.

With that in mind, I will tell you how Bitcoin ETFs can offer a safer, more accessible way (for many people) to include this powerful asset in your wealth-building journey.

What Do I Do with Bitcoin?

As I've mentioned many times already, this book is not another copy-paste from the internet. I don't believe in creating long lists of investments I've never touched or strategies I've never tried. The world is already full of those "guides" written by people who only Googled their content but never put it into practice. That's not what you'll find here.

What I share in this book comes from **real-world experience** — the things I've tested, lived through, succeeded with, and sometimes even failed at. That's why, for example, when I spoke about gold earlier, I admitted that while it's a great wealth preserver and hedge against inflation, I'm not personally a fan of it as an investment strategy for financial freedom. I told you why.

But Bitcoin is different. I **am** a fan of Bitcoin — not blindly, not emotionally, but because of its **remarkable potential.** Yes, it is volatile. Yes, it crashes. But if you learn how to approach it properly, those same crashes can actually work **for you**, not against you. While many panic and sell at a loss, you can see those dips as opportunities — as discounted entry points into one of the fastest-growing wealth containers of our lifetime.

I'll explain exactly how I personally approach Bitcoin: how I manage the risks, how I take advantage of the volatility instead of being hurt by it, and how you can use it as a tool — not a gamble — on your journey toward financial freedom.

Before I show you how I invest in Bitcoin...

Before I reveal exactly how I invest in Bitcoin — in my simplified, practical way that anyone can follow — I first need to tell you about something equally important: **Bitcoin ETFs.**

Why? Because I personally invest in **both** Bitcoin itself and in Bitcoin ETFs. And for many people, ETFs can actually be the safer, easier, and more accessible way to get started.

You see, one of the biggest challenges with Bitcoin has always been the technical side: digital wallets, private keys, exchanges, and the constant fear of losing access if you forget a password. This has stopped countless people from ever touching Bitcoin, even though they're interested in it.

But now, thanks to the creation of Bitcoin ETFs, you don't have to deal with any of that complexity. You can invest in Bitcoin the same way you invest in stocks or index funds — through a normal brokerage account. No wallets, no passwords, no private keys to manage. Just buy and hold, like you would with any other ETF.

This innovation has completely changed the game. It's made Bitcoin accessible not just to tech-savvy traders but to **everyone** — students, retirees, business owners, even an 80-year-old grandma. That's why before I show you my exact Bitcoin strategy, you need to understand how these ETFs work, and why they matter.

Even if you feel uncertain about using brokers, there's another option you can trust: **your bank.** These days, almost every major bank has its own investment platform, where you can open an account and buy stocks, ETFs, index funds, and more. For example, here in Canada, every large bank offers this service, and I'm sure the same is true in the United States and many other countries.

It's simple: you sign up for an investment account with the same bank you already use, transfer money into it, and then choose from their wide directory of investments. This way, you don't need to worry about whether some online broker is trustworthy — you're working with your bank, which you already know and trust.

However, here's something important to understand: **banks generally don't sell Bitcoin directly.** At least, I've never seen a bank that allows you to log into your online account and buy actual Bitcoin. What they do offer, though, is a variety of ETFs — including **Bitcoin ETFs.** These ETFs are listed alongside regular stock market investments, and you can buy and hold them in exactly the same way.

If you want to buy Bitcoin itself, you'll still need to use a cryptocurrency broker such as Coinbase, Binance, or another exchange. But if you take this route, make sure the broker you choose is **regulated in your country** and operates under government supervision. That extra layer of protection is vital when dealing with something as new and fast-moving as cryptocurrency.

What Are Bitcoin ETFs?

There is one more thing that I must explain to complete this long introduction and then tell you how I invest in Bitcoin: **What Are Bitcoin ETFs?**

An ETF, or **Exchange-Traded Fund**, is simply an investment fund that's traded on stock exchanges, just like a regular stock. Instead of buying the asset directly, you buy shares of the ETF, which represent ownership of that asset.

So, a **Bitcoin ETF** is a fund that holds Bitcoin (or Bitcoin-related contracts), and when you buy shares of that ETF, you're indirectly investing in Bitcoin without ever touching a crypto wallet, private keys, or exchanges. It looks and feels just like buying any stock or index fund through your bank or broker.

Types of Bitcoin ETFs

1. Spot Bitcoin ETFs

A spot Bitcoin ETF actually holds Bitcoin. For every share of the ETF, there's real Bitcoin backing it, stored safely by the fund managers. This means your ETF shares rise and fall almost exactly in line with the price of Bitcoin itself. Spot ETFs are the closest thing to owning Bitcoin without the hassle of managing it yourself.

2. Futures Bitcoin ETFs

A futures Bitcoin ETF doesn't hold real Bitcoin. Instead, it invests in **futures contracts** — agreements to buy or sell Bitcoin at a future date. These ETFs try to track Bitcoin's price, but they don't always match perfectly, and they often come with higher fees and risks. They're more complex and usually better suited to traders than long-term investors.

Why Spot Bitcoin ETFs Are Safer for Investors

If your goal is financial freedom and long-term wealth, **spot Bitcoin ETFs are the better choice.** Here's why:

- They are **simpler** — directly tied to the actual Bitcoin price.
- They are **transparent** — each share is backed by real Bitcoin.
- They are **more cost-efficient** — usually with lower fees than futures ETFs.
- They are **less risky** — no need to worry about rolling futures contracts, which can eat into returns.

In short, a spot Bitcoin ETF gives you the upside of Bitcoin with the safety and convenience of buying a regular stock or index fund.

Now... here's exactly how I invest in Bitcoin.

1. I buy every month, no matter the price.

Each month, I purchase a small amount of Bitcoin through a regulated, trusted broker. I pick a specific day of the month and stick to it. This way, the price doesn't matter — whether it's high or low, I keep buying. Occasionally, if I see Bitcoin has dropped significantly within that month, I might add a little extra, but that happens rarely.

2. I buy and forget.

Once I buy, I don't obsess over the account. I don't check daily profits or losses. Why? Because this is a **long-term investment.** The short-term ups and downs don't matter when you're focused on the big picture.

3. I invest only 1–2% of my income.

Here's the golden rule: never invest more than **1–2% of your monthly active income** in Bitcoin. For example, if you earn $1,000 per month, you should only put $10–$20 into Bitcoin. This keeps the risk tiny and manageable.

4. I treat crashes as opportunities.

When Bitcoin drops by **25% or more,** instead of panicking, I add another 1–2%. Most people sell in fear — that's why they lose. But if you stay calm, crashes become discounts, not disasters.

5. I never let greed take over.

When Bitcoin is skyrocketing, it's tempting to throw in 20% of your income because you feel like you're missing out. Don't do it. Every big upward run is followed by a strong correction. If you over-invest at the top, you'll regret it. Stick to 1–2% per month. That's the only real "secret" — and it's simple enough that anyone can follow it.

By following this extremely simple — yet wise — strategy, the results I've seen have been incredible. Not because I gamble or take huge risks, but because I stay **consistent, disciplined, and patient.** That's exactly how Bitcoin can become a powerful tool in your journey to financial freedom.

Once again, remember this: the Bitcoin market can be extremely risky if you take **unreasonable risks.** Don't let this amazing opportunity turn into a disaster by making careless mistakes — especially by investing too much too quickly. Consistency and caution are your strongest allies.

What About Bitcoin ETFs?

Alongside buying real Bitcoin, I also invest in a **Bitcoin ETF** that I found on my bank's investment platform — a cheap and well-backed Canadian spot Bitcoin ETF. And I treat it the same way I treat my direct Bitcoin purchases: I buy regularly and hold for the long term.

You may ask: *Why bother with the ETF if I'm already buying real Bitcoin? Isn't one enough?*
The answer is simple: **safety.**

Think of the Bitcoin ETF as my **life jacket.**

I buy real Bitcoin through a regulated broker, which is fine most of the time. But brokers, no matter how large or well-known, carry risks. What if they go bankrupt? What if they get hacked? What if one day I can't log into my account, and support doesn't help? While regulators may step in to protect customers, there's no guarantee how quickly or fully those problems would be resolved.

That's why I also buy Bitcoin ETFs through my bank. Banks don't sell actual Bitcoin directly — at least, I've never seen one that does — but they do offer ETFs. And I trust my bank much more than any broker. The ETF rises when Bitcoin rises, and it falls when Bitcoin falls. So, if Bitcoin's price goes up, I profit whether I hold the coin itself or the ETF

This combination gives me the best of both worlds:

- The **pure exposure** of owning real Bitcoin directly.
- The **safety net** of holding an ETF inside my bank account, under strict financial regulations.

It's a simple system, but it works. If you're uncomfortable with the risks of working through brokers, you could even skip buying real Bitcoin altogether and stick with a **Bitcoin ETF** instead. That way, your investment remains entirely under the security of your bank.

Personally, I do both. Because I only ever invest **1–2% of my monthly income** into real Bitcoin, and because I use a well-regulated broker, I'm not worried. Still, I see the ETF as an added layer of protection. Over time, real Bitcoin has the potential to outperform ETFs, but the ETF offers peace of mind. In the end, it's up to you to weigh the risks and rewards and decide which approach feels right for your own journey.

If you want to do the same as I do, remember: you should only invest **1–2% of your monthly active income** in the Bitcoin ETF as well. The same discipline and rules I explained for buying real Bitcoin apply here too. Consistency and moderation are key.

Also note that your bank's investment platform may list several different Bitcoin ETFs. Don't get confused and try to buy them all. You only need **one** — and the best choice is the one that:

- Has been around for a longer time (proven track record).
- Charges lower fees and its price is also lower than the others (cheaper).
- Is a **spot Bitcoin ETF** (backed by real Bitcoin, not futures contracts).

Another important detail is **currency exchange costs.** Many banks allow you to buy not only domestic ETFs, but also foreign ones. For example, here in Canada, my bank's investment platform gives me access to plenty of U.S. stocks and ETFs. But I avoid them, because every time I buy or sell, I lose money on the **currency conversion** between Canadian dollars (CAD) and U.S. dollars (USD).

Yes, I could keep both CAD and USD balances in my investment account, but for the sake of **simplicity and efficiency**, I stick to Canadian ETFs only. This way, I don't have to worry about hidden exchange fees eating into my profits.

So, if you're in the United States and your bank's platform offers Canadian ETFs, the same warning applies to you. Be careful about exchange costs, and keep your investments in your **home currency** whenever possible. That's one of those small details that make a big difference over the long term.

Final Notes on Bitcoin

Bitcoin is not a magic ticket, nor is it a reckless gamble if approached wisely. It's simply another tool — one that, when handled with **discipline, consistency, and patience,** can help preserve and grow your wealth over time.

The secret is simple: buy small, buy regularly, and never risk more than 1–2% of your active income each month. Treat the crashes as opportunities, not disasters. And if you want an extra layer of safety, add a **spot Bitcoin ETF** through your bank alongside your direct Bitcoin holdings. This combination gives you both growth potential and peace of mind.

Just remember: Bitcoin should never be your only investment, nor should it dominate your financial strategy. It's one piece of the puzzle. A powerful piece, yes — but only when it's used with care.

Now that we've covered real estate, gold, stocks, index funds, and Bitcoin, let's move on to the next opportunity. The journey isn't over yet — in fact, some of the most practical and reliable investment methods are still ahead.

6. Bonds

When you hear the word *bond*, think of it as a **loan that you give to a government or a company.** Instead of you borrowing money from the bank, this time you are the one lending money — and in return, they pay you interest. That interest is your **passive income.**

For example, if you buy a government bond, you're basically lending money to your government. They promise to pay you back the full amount on a certain date (called the **maturity date**) plus regular interest payments along the way. With corporate bonds, it works the same way, except you are lending money to a company instead of the government.

Why Bonds Matter for Financial Freedom

Unlike stocks or Bitcoin, bonds aren't meant to make you rich quickly. Their power lies in **stability and predictability.** You know in advance how much interest you'll earn and when you'll get your money back. This makes bonds a valuable part of your financial freedom journey because they:

- Give you **steady passive income** through interest payments.
- Protect your portfolio from big swings in riskier assets.
- Let you sleep peacefully, knowing your money is backed (especially with government bonds).

Types of Bonds

1. **Government Bonds**
   - The safest kind of bonds, because they're backed by governments.
   - Examples: U.S. Treasury Bonds, Canadian Government Bonds.
   - Lower risk = lower return, but very reliable.

2. **Corporate Bonds**
   - Issued by companies to raise money.
   - Pay higher interest than government bonds, but carry more risk (companies can fail).
   - Big, stable companies (like banks or utilities) are usually safer issuers than small or struggling businesses.

How to Invest in Bonds

The good news is, you don't need to be a financial expert to buy bonds. You can:

- **Use your bank's investment platform** — most major banks let you buy government and corporate bonds directly.
- **Buy bond ETFs** — instead of owning one single bond, you buy a basket of them through an ETF, which is safer and easier for beginners.

When you invest, pay attention to two things:

1. **Maturity date** (how long until you get your money back).
2. **Interest rate** (the percentage you'll earn).

Pros and Cons of Bonds

Pros:

- Safe and reliable.
- Predictable passive income.
- Good protection against stock market crashes.

Cons:

- Lower returns compared to stocks or Bitcoin.
- Inflation can eat into your profit (if inflation is higher than your bond's interest rate, you're actually losing purchasing power).
- Some corporate bonds can still default (fail to pay back).

My Advice on Bonds

Start simple. If you're new, stick with **government bonds** or a **bond ETF from your bank's platform.** Don't chase high-risk corporate bonds promising big returns — that's how beginners get burned. Remember, bonds are not here to make you rich; they are here to **protect your money and give you steady income** while your other investments (like stocks or Bitcoin) work harder for growth.

7. Savings Accounts with Interest

Not all investments need to be complicated. Sometimes the simplest ones are the safest — and that's where **savings accounts with interest** come in. These include products like:

- **GICs (Guaranteed Investment Certificates)** in Canada
- **CDs (Certificates of Deposit)** in the United States
- **Fixed deposits / time deposits** in many other countries
- Or even **high-interest savings accounts (HISAs)** offered by your local bank

No matter what they're called where you live, the principle is the same: **you give your money to the bank for a certain period, and in return, the bank pays you interest.**

How They Work

1. **Fixed-Term Products (like GICs/CDs):**

- You deposit your money for a set period (for example, 6 months, 1 year, or 5 years).
- The bank pays you a guaranteed interest rate.
- At the end of the term (called maturity), you get your original money back plus the interest.

2. **High-Interest Savings Accounts (HISAs):**

- You can withdraw your money anytime.
- Interest rates are usually lower than fixed-term products.
- Useful for building an emergency fund while still earning something.

Why They Matter in Your Financial Freedom Journey

Savings accounts with interest are not going to make you rich — but they **protect your money** and give you a steady, predictable return. They are perfect for:

- Building a **safe foundation** for your investments.
- Parking money you don't want to risk in stocks or Bitcoin.
- Having quick access to cash if you need it (especially in HISAs).
- Sleeping peacefully at night, knowing your money is insured (in Canada, CDIC insures GICs up to a limit; in the U.S., FDIC insures CDs and savings accounts).

Pros and Cons

Pros

- Very safe — often insured by government programs.
- Guaranteed return, no surprises.
- Good for short-term goals and capital protection.

Cons

- Low returns compared to stocks, real estate, or Bitcoin.
- Inflation often grows faster than your interest, meaning your purchasing power may still shrink over time.

- Fixed-term products lock your money — you may pay a penalty if you withdraw early.

My Advice

I don't recommend putting all your money here, because low returns won't make you financially free. But I do recommend keeping a **portion of your wealth** in these accounts for safety and liquidity. For example:

- Keep your **emergency fund** in a high-interest savings account.
- Use GICs/CDs/fixed deposits for money you want to protect and grow slowly.

Think of this as your **safety cushion** — not your wealth builder.

How to Open a Savings Account with Interest

The good news is — this is one of the easiest investments you'll ever make.

1. **Start with Your Bank**
   Go to your bank (or credit union) and simply ask: *"What savings products with guaranteed interest do you offer?"* They'll explain their options — whether it's a high-interest savings account, a GIC (Canada), a CD (U.S.), or a fixed deposit (other countries).

2. **Check Online**
   Most banks list these products clearly on their websites, along with the current interest rates, minimum deposits, and terms (6 months, 1 year, 5 years, etc.).

3. **Negotiate for a Better Deal**
   Here's a tip: if the bank sees you're ready to invest a **larger amount** or commit for a **longer term,** they may offer you a better rate. Don't be shy to ask, *"Can you give me a higher rate if I lock this in for longer?"*

4. **Keep It Simple**
   You don't need a financial advisor, a broker, or complicated paperwork. These accounts are straightforward, government-backed in most countries, and designed to be safe and easy for everyone.

These accounts won't make you rich, but they give you **security and stability** — two things every financial freedom plan needs. Use them for your emergency fund, or as the "safe" portion of your portfolio. They may not generate high returns, but they allow you to **protect your capital while your other investments — like stocks, index funds, or real estate — do the heavy lifting.**

You may have heard about mutual funds. While they can provide diversification, I don't recommend them for most people because they usually come with higher fees and lower returns compared to index funds or ETFs. That's why I've focused on index funds in this book — they give you the same benefits, but cheaper, simpler, and more effective.

What Next? Creating Your Own Financial Freedom Plan

Now you've learned about all the investment methods — real estate, gold, stocks, index funds, Bitcoin, bonds, and savings accounts with interest. But here's the big question: **how do you put it all together?**

The answer is to create a simple **allocation plan**: decide how much of your monthly savings (from your active income) should go into each category. This way, you're not gambling on one single investment — you're building a strong, diversified foundation.

My Suggested Allocation Plan

Here's a sample plan you can start with. Of course, you can adjust it depending on your income, your risk tolerance, and your personal goals

- **Real Estate: 30–40%**

    This is the long-term cornerstone of wealth. It requires more savings and patience, but over time, real estate generates strong passive income and builds real assets.

- **Dividend Stocks & Index Funds: 25–35%**

    These give you growth, diversification, and passive income through dividends. They're easier to start with than real estate and can be scaled automatically over time.

- **Bonds & Savings Accounts with Interest: 15–20%**

    These are your safety net. They won't make you rich, but they protect your capital, balance your portfolio, and let you sleep peacefully at night.

- **Bitcoin (and Bitcoin ETFs): 1–2% per month of your income**

    This is your "high potential" investment. By keeping it small and consistent, you benefit from Bitcoin's long-term growth without risking too much.

- **Gold: 5–10%**

    Gold doesn't create passive income, but it preserves wealth and protects you against inflation. It's your insurance policy against uncertainty.

Why This Works

This plan balances **growth, safety, and opportunity.**

- Real estate and dividend stocks create consistent passive income
- Index funds give you broad, long-term growth.
- Bonds and savings accounts protect your wealth.

- Bitcoin gives you exposure to high upside.
- Gold secures your purchasing power.

The exact percentages aren't as important as the **discipline of sticking to your plan.** Over time, this diversified approach creates the snowball effect that leads to financial freedom.

You also don't need to feel locked into the exact percentages I suggested. If putting 30–40% of your income toward real estate feels too heavy right now, lower it. Maybe you start with 10–15% instead and build up over time. The important thing is that you're **investing something, consistently**, in the core wealth-building categories. Flexibility is part of the plan — you adjust the numbers to fit your lifestyle and comfort level, but you never stop the habit of investing.

Do You Have to Invest in All of Them?

The short answer is **No**.

Financial freedom isn't about spreading yourself thin across every single option. It's about finding the methods that are both profitable and practical for you. Some investments are absolutely worth doing, while others can be skipped if they don't fit your personality, lifestyle, or goals.

The Best Core Investments

If you want to simplify and still build a strong path to financial freedom, focus on these first:

- **Dividend Stocks & Index Funds** — These are my top recommendations. They're easy to start, can be fully automated, and create real passive income.

- **Real Estate** — If you can save enough for a 30% down payment, real estate becomes the ultimate long-term wealth builder. It's harder to start but incredibly powerful over decades.
- **Bitcoin (1–2% per month)** — Not a "must," but I highly recommend having at least some exposure. It's the future of wealth storage, and if you do it with discipline, it can be life-

changing.

- **Bonds & Savings Accounts** — These are your safety cushion. They won't make you rich, but they protect you and give you stability when other investments are volatile.

Investments You Can Skip (Optional)

- **Gold** — Gold is a solid store of value, but it doesn't generate passive income. If you'd rather focus on investments that *pay you dividends* or *grow automatically,* you can skip gold without hurting your journey.

- **Anything Too Complex** — If an investment feels confusing or you don't fully understand it, skip it. As I said earlier, never invest in something you don't understand.

You don't need to invest in everything. Even if you just focus on **stocks (dividend + index funds), real estate, and a small portion of Bitcoin** — while keeping some savings in safe accounts or bonds — you'll already have one of the strongest financial freedom plans possible.

The key is not to try everything, but to **do a few things consistently and well.**

An Example: Turning $5,000 a Month Into Millions

Let's imagine this together.

You're earning **$5,000 each month** from your job or online business. Instead of spending it all, you decide to follow the plan I've outlined in this book. Month after month, you commit to putting aside money into the four core areas that build real financial freedom:

- **Real Estate (30%)** (saving toward down payments and growing rental income)

- **Dividend Stocks & Index Funds (30%)** (building a portfolio that pays you)
- **Bonds & Savings Accounts (15%)** (your safety net)
- **Bitcoin (2%)** (your high-potential growth bet)

After 10 Years

Your discipline starts to pay off. You've managed to buy at least **one rental apartment**, which covers its mortgage through rent and still leaves you with some positive cash flow. Your stock and index fund portfolio has grown steadily, paying you dividends along the way. Bitcoin — even though you only put 1–2% of your income into it each month — has grown enough to become a meaningful part of your wealth. Altogether, your consistent investing has built you around **$700,000 in assets:**

- Real Estate Fund: ~$246K
- Stocks/Index Funds: ~$274K
- Bonds/Savings: ~$105K
- Bitcoin: ~$38K

After 20 Years

This is where the snowball really begins to roll. Your real estate investments have doubled (or even tripled) in value, while also giving you steady rental income. Your dividend stocks and index funds are much larger now, and the dividends they pay could easily cover many of your monthly expenses. Bitcoin, with all its ups and downs, has grown dramatically compared to what you first put in. At this stage, your portfolio could be worth about **$2.2 million:**

- Real Estate Fund: ~$693K
- Stocks/Index Funds: ~$884K
- Bonds/Savings: ~$246K
- Bitcoin: ~$311K

After 30 Years

This is financial freedom, plain and simple. Your rental income alone could cover all your living costs. Your stocks and index funds are sending you dividend checks that feel like a second salary. Your bonds and savings give you stability, and Bitcoin — if you stayed disciplined — has rewarded you far beyond what most people would expect. Altogether, your total wealth could now exceed **$6.4 million.**

- Real Estate Fund: ~$1.51M
- Stocks/Index Funds: ~$2.24M
- Bonds/Savings: ~$437K
- Bitcoin: ~$2.30M

What This Means

- You didn't get here by taking wild risks — you got here by **consistent monthly investing** across a few proven categories.
- Real estate and stocks are the backbone of this portfolio.
- Bonds and savings accounts don't grow as much but give you **stability and safety**.
- Bitcoin starts tiny, but after 10 years, it's big enough to matter without ever risking too much of your income.

The Lesson

- **Stocks & Index Funds + Real Estate** make up the bulk of your long-term wealth.
- **Bitcoin**, even at just 2% monthly, becomes a massive contributor over decades — showing why discipline matters.
- **Bonds & Savings** don't grow as aggressively, but they provide safety and balance.

Notice something important here: you didn't gamble, you didn't chase every hot trend, and you didn't need to risk everything. You simply saved consistently, diversified wisely, and gave your money time to work for you.

That's the formula for financial freedom. It's not about luck or timing. It's about **discipline, patience, and consistency.**

Do you remember the story of the cleaning lady?

In the example above, I assumed you make $5,000 in active income. But our cleaning lady earned far less than that — yet she still achieved financial freedom, early retirement, and a reasonable level of wealth. How? Simply by focusing on one thing she trusted: real estate. She didn't know about stocks, bonds, or Bitcoin, but she didn't need to. With nothing more than discipline, dedication, and patience, she built her freedom. That's the lesson for you too: even if you choose just one path, as long as you stick with it consistently, your future can be far brighter than you might imagine.

Financial freedom doesn't require a high income — even modest earnings, when paired with discipline, patience, and consistency, can snowball into wealth over time.

You don't need to use every method I covered. The cleaning lady only used real estate, and it still worked for her. But, if you combine multiple paths with a higher income, you can do even better than she did.

Closing Thoughts for Chapter 4

Financial freedom isn't built in a day, and it isn't built by luck. It's built brick by brick, habit by habit, choice by choice. You've now learned how to take the money you earn and put it to work — in real estate, stocks, index funds, bonds, or even Bitcoin. The exact mix you choose matters less than the discipline you bring to it. Remember, wealth isn't about chasing the next big thing; it's about consistency, patience, and faith in the process.

The key is to **start where you are, with what you have, and trust the journey**. Even small amounts, invested wisely and repeatedly, will grow into something life-changing. Your money can now begin working for you, day and night, while you focus on living the life you want.

With this foundation in place, we're ready to turn the page to Chapter 5 — where I'll share some final, timeless pieces of advice that will keep you on track, protect you from the common traps, and help you stay steady on your journey toward lasting freedom.

Chapter 5
Wisdom for the Journey

You've now learned how to build active income, transform it into passive income, and create a system that steadily moves you toward financial freedom. But knowledge alone isn't enough. What determines your success in the long run is the wisdom you carry with you — the principles, mindset, and discipline that guide every decision you make from this point forward.

This chapter isn't about new strategies or technical details. It's about the timeless lessons that protect you from mistakes, keep you grounded during storms, and remind you why you started this journey in the first place. Think of it as your compass — wisdom for the journey that never goes out of style.

1. Choose Your Hard

Living poor is hard. Achieving financial freedom is hard. **Choose your hard.**

What you've learned in this book so far may make you think that achieving financial freedom — even in the simple, step-by-step way I've introduced — is hard. And you're right. It's not easy. It takes time, discipline, and sacrifice. But here's the real question: *is living poor any easier?*

Living poor is its own kind of hard. Struggling to provide for yourself and your loved ones. Working until the last day of your life because you can't afford to stop. Worrying every month about rent, bills, or whether you can take even a short break without falling behind. That is hard. Much harder than building wealth.

At least with financial freedom, the "hard" you choose is temporary. You work, you sacrifice, you stay disciplined for a few years — and then you're free. But the "hard" of poverty never ends. It follows you, day after day, year after year, unless you choose differently.

So yes, both paths are hard. But only one leads to freedom. **Make the choice today: endure the temporary hard work of building financial freedom, instead of the lifelong struggle of living without it.** The effort you put in now will give you a life where money no longer controls you — and that's a hard worth choosing.

2. Avoid Get-Rich-Quick Schemes

Wealth is never built through get-rich-quick schemes — because they aren't designed to make *you* rich. They are designed to make the **founders** of the schemes rich.

On your journey to financial freedom, you will be tempted by countless shiny offers that promise to shorten the path and save you time. They will look attractive, urgent, and easy. But chasing them is one of the biggest mistakes you can make. At best, you will waste precious time and money. At worst, you will lose everything you've worked so hard to build.

Unless you win the lottery or inherit a fortune overnight, there are no shortcuts to wealth. It must be built **brick by brick, choice by choice, day by day.**

And remember — running an illegitimate scheme yourself, whether a Ponzi program, a pyramid setup, or a crypto rug-pull, won't make you wealthy either. It won't bring you financial freedom — it will bring you handcuffs.

True wealth is quiet, patient, and built on solid ground. Every time you reject a shortcut, you strengthen the discipline that will carry you all the way to freedom.

Remember this rule for life: *If it sounds too good to be true, it always is.*

3. Dealing with Trolls and Devils

Nothing is worse than crossing paths with a truly toxic person in business or life. If your source of active income involves people — for example, running a website, building an online community, or offering services — you will inevitably encounter them. Thankfully, they are not the majority, but even a single one each year can feel like too many.

These people come in many forms: trolls who call you a scam for no reason, strangers who leave false or damaging reviews, bullies who send hostile messages, and manipulators who even threaten lawsuits or demand money to avoid "ruining" your reputation. They thrive on intimidation and negativity. My own inbox has been filled with these kinds of messages over the years, and I know how discouraging they can be —if you take them personally.

The first thing you must remember is this: **never take it personally.** What these people do is not about you — it's about them. They are full of hate, resentment, and unresolved pain from their own past. Wherever they go, they create problems, and you just happen to be their next target.

Trying to talk to them or explain yourself only makes it worse. They see it as a sign of weakness, proof that you're afraid, and that they can push you into giving them what they want.

It doesn't matter who the person is — it could even be someone close to you, like a spouse or family member. The moment you recognize that they are abusive, manipulative, or filled with hate, you must **step out of their way and cut communication.** At most, you can respond once, politely and professionally, to see if the situation calms down. But if the abuse continues — if they send nasty emails, post slander, or try to sabotage your work — you must block them, ban them, and move on.

Always keep records: save their emails, take screenshots of their posts and threats, and document names. email addresses, and even IP addresses if you can. This protects you if the situation escalates. In nearly all cases, when you ignore them and stop feeding their game, they vanish. If you keep engaging, you'll end up in a never-ending ping-pong match that drains your energy.

And don't let their threats scare you. They might leave a bad review or throw around words like "lawsuit," but the truth is they almost never follow through. People are smart enough to recognize false reviews for what they are. And real lawsuits cost money and effort — things trolls rarely invest.

The only exception is if you ever receive a **serious threat to your life or safety.** That is rare, but if it happens, keep every piece of evidence and immediately report it to the police.

4. Dealing with Energy Vampires

Energy vampires may not look as dangerous as trolls, but in reality, they can be far more harmful. With trolls, if you follow the steps I outlined earlier — cutting them off, blocking them, documenting their actions — they usually disappear and never come back. But energy vampires are different. They don't always attack directly, and that's what makes them dangerous.

Sometimes, they are the people closest to you — parents, siblings, relatives, friends, even a spouse. Because they don't appear aggressive on the surface, you might tolerate them, thinking their behavior is harmless. But make no mistake: **the negativity they drip into your life can slowly destroy your energy, your confidence, and your future.**

Energy vampires are often deeply wounded inside, just like trolls. But they are more subtle. They may not shout or attack, but they know exactly when to whisper a cutting remark, raise a doubt, or say the one thing that collapses your confidence at the worst possible moment. They sense your weaknesses, and they feed on them.

Many of these people show narcissistic traits — they feel defective and insecure because of damage they suffered early in life. And yes, some trolls fall into this category too. But energy vampires are harder to spot because they hide behind charm, politeness, or even love. That's why you must be extra vigilant.

If you identify someone in your life who constantly drains your energy, undermines your confidence, or plants negativity in your mind, you must act decisively. **Distance yourself. Protect your mind. Guard your energy.** No dream, no business, and no journey toward financial freedom can survive if you let energy vampires stay in your inner circle.

If you live with an energy vampire, or have one among your closest circle, you must accept a hard truth: **you will not achieve your dreams as long as they remain in your life.** Most people are not strong enough to ignore these toxic influences. They internalize the poison, and the damage can last for years — even a lifetime.

I know this firsthand. For years, I had such people around me. One of them, now a 70-year-old man, was deeply traumatized as a child after being raped multiple times at the age of nine and after. His parents kicked him out of the house when he was just nine, and he ended up working and living among people, some of whom were extremely abusive. As a result, he grew into the very definition of a narcissist, psychopath, and borderline personality. No living being was safe from his behavior. At times, I became his target too. Eventually, I learned to ignore him, and later, to cut him out of my life completely.

Over time, I realized that others I had considered my "closest supporters" were no different — they were enemies in disguise, carrying darkness inside them. They injected negativity at the worst possible moments, sabotaging progress with their words and actions.

Energy vampires often live in a state of constant misery, convinced they are unlucky and doomed. Their negativity doesn't just drain your energy — it spreads like a curse, affecting your mindset, your opportunities, even your sense of hope for the future. **If you are serious about achieving financial freedom and building wealth, you must remove these people from your life completely.**

It may feel harsh, but once you do, you will experience something almost miraculous: a lightness, a freedom, and new opportunities opening before you. Prosperity thrives where there is clarity, peace, and positive energy. But it cannot survive in the presence of poison. *The doors of wealth open only when you shut the doors to toxicity.*

5. Avoid Bad-Luck People

That title may sound strange, and you might ask: *Who are "bad-luck people," and how can you recognize them?*

They are the ones who constantly believe they are unlucky — that success, wealth, and happiness are reserved for others, not for them. Their mindset is toxic, and the dangerous part is this: **they can transfer it to you.** Spend enough time with them, and before you know it, you'll start thinking the same way.

Avoid such people as you would rabid dogs or poisonous snakes. If that belief system takes root in your mind, your life begins sliding downhill. Nothing will seem to work, and no matter how hard you try, failure will feel inevitable.

The quality of your life depends directly on the quality of your thoughts. Positive, empowered, and resilient thoughts lead you upward toward your dreams. Negative, hopeless, and self-defeating thoughts drag you downward. And nothing shapes your mindset more than the people around you.

It's simple:

- **If you surround yourself with five wealthy, motivated, and successful people, you will likely become the sixth.**
- **If you surround yourself with five "losers" who see themselves as unlucky, doomed, and powerless, you will also become the sixth.**

So choose wisely. Your circle either pulls you up or drags you down — there is no neutral.

If everyone — or even most people — around you carry this toxic "bad-luck" mindset, then you must step away from all of them and start an independent life. **Being alone is far better than being surrounded by people who poison your thoughts and drain your future — no matter who they are.**

I once knew a man who had lived for decades under communist beliefs. He believed — and repeated often — that if you fail in business, you will *never* be able to get back up. That, of course, is a lie. History is filled with examples of the world's most successful people who went bankrupt more than once, only to come back stronger.

But this man embodied his belief. He lived as the ultimate example of failure. Always broke, always in debt, never able to pay rent, and constantly cheating even the people closest to him. Lying and manipulation had become his way of life. And worse, he spread this mentality to everyone around him. In the end, he died poor, broken, miserable, and damned. That is what a toxic mindset does — it destroys not just wealth, but also dignity and relationships.

In contrast, I also know people with the opposite mindset. They radiate positivity, work ethic, and resilience. Even when they fail, they treat failure as a lesson, then restart with more strength and wisdom. Life consistently rewards them. When you meet people like this, you don't just hear their words — you *feel* their energy. Their character and aura naturally inspire confidence, hope, and action.

Find these people. Surround yourself with them. And if you can't find them right away, **become one of them.** Live with positivity, discipline, and resilience, and soon you'll attract the same kind of successful, like-minded people into your life.

Your circle is your future. Choose it wisely — because who you walk with will decide how far you go.

6. Health First

No amount of money, no level of success, and no milestone of financial freedom is worth it if your health is gone. Too many people make the mistake of working so hard for wealth that they sacrifice the very body and mind that are supposed to enjoy it. That is not freedom—it's another form of slavery.

Financial freedom requires consistency, energy, and focus. You can't stay consistent if you are always tired, burned out, or ill. Just as you must learn to manage your money wisely, you must learn to manage your body and mind with the same discipline.

Here are a few guiding principles to help you stay balanced:

1. **Rest and Sleep**
   You wouldn't expect a car to run endlessly without fuel. Your body is no different. Sleep is where recovery happens—mentally, emotionally, and physically. If you want sharp decisions and the patience required to follow your financial plan, guard your sleep like your wealth depends on it—because it does.

2. **Movement Is Medicine**
   You don't have to be a marathon runner or bodybuilder. But you must move daily. A short walk, stretching, or a simple home

workout keeps your energy levels high and your stress levels low. Sitting endlessly at a desk or in front of charts will shorten your life, not lengthen your wealth.

3. **Eat Like an Investor**
   Every meal is an investment in your future self. Junk food is like a bad financial habit: it feels good now but costs you more later. Choose food that fuels your brain and strengthens your body. Think of your diet as compound interest for your health.

4. **Protect Your Mind**
   Stress, toxic people, and endless worry will age you faster than time itself. Just as you filter your financial investments, filter what you let into your mind. Surround yourself with positive influences, practice mindfulness or prayer, and don't let every setback weigh you down.

5. **Routine Health Checks**
   A great investor doesn't just hope everything is fine—they check, measure, and adjust. Your body deserves the same respect. Regular medical check-ups are like reviewing your portfolio—they prevent small problems from becoming disasters.

Remember: you are building wealth not just for the sake of money, but for the life money makes possible. That life loses all meaning if you don't have the health to enjoy it. **True financial freedom is being able to wake up every day with energy, clarity, and peace of mind—ready to live, not just survive.**

7. Choose a Mentor

As you've seen, the journey to financial freedom is all about following the right people and learning from the right examples. The best way to shorten your learning curve is to have a mentor — someone whose wisdom, discipline, and results speak louder than any theory.

If you ask me who the greatest mentor is for anyone seeking financial freedom, my answer is simple: **Warren Buffett**. Not only is he the living legend of investing, but he is also the embodiment of humility, patience, and character. His life and words are proof that financial success is built on discipline, long-term thinking, and avoiding foolish risks.

The good news is, you don't need to sit down with him or attend a private class. His teachings are everywhere — in books, interviews, videos, and timeless quotes. They are more than enough to guide you if you take them seriously. The key is to keep reminding yourself of his principles and to actually apply them in your daily financial decisions. A mentor doesn't just inspire you; a mentor keeps you on track when you're tempted to take shortcuts.

Here are some of Buffett's quotes that have helped me enormously. I know them by heart, and I repeat them to myself often — because they are simple, practical, and powerful reminders to stay on track.

1. "If you don't find a way to make money while you sleep, you will work until you die."

This is the very first principle you should memorize and follow. It explains why you must force your *active income* to generate *passive income*. Passive income is the money that flows in even while you're asleep, and without it, financial freedom is impossible.

2. "If you buy things you don't need, soon you will have to sell things you need."

This is Buffett's timeless warning against waste and the trap of "looking rich" instead of *becoming rich*. Your hard-earned money should be put to work building assets, not spent on unnecessary luxuries. I already emphasized this earlier in the book: avoid trying to impress others. Looking wealthy is temporary. Building wealth is forever.

3. "If you can't control your emotions, you can't control your money."

Financial freedom requires discipline. If you panic during downturns or chase hype when markets rise, you'll sabotage your own wealth. Emotional control is the key to staying consistent with your plan.

4. "An idiot with a plan can beat a genius without one."

You don't need to be a financial genius — you just need a clear plan and the patience to follow it. A simple savings-and-investing plan executed consistently beats brilliant but undisciplined guesses.

5. "It's insane to risk what you have for what you don't need."

Never gamble your financial security for unnecessary gains. Protect your foundation first — once you're financially free, you don't need to risk it all chasing more.

6. "Be fearful when others are greedy, and greedy when others are fearful."

Most people do the opposite: they buy at the top and sell at the bottom. Financial freedom comes when you train yourself to think differently — patience and courage when others panic.

7. "Wealth is the transfer of money from impatient to patient."

Those who chase shortcuts lose to those who wait. Compounding only works for people who give it time. The patient investor wins in the end.

8. "If you find yourself in a hole, stop digging."

If a financial decision isn't working, don't double down. Pause, reassess and protect your capital. The first rule is to stop losses before they grow

9. "You can't buy time. It's the one the rich and poor spend equally."

Money can multiply, but time cannot. Start now. Every year you wait delays the compounding effect that builds true wealth.

10. "You will move in the direction of the people that you associate with. So it's important to associate with people that are better than yourself."

Surround yourself with people who think big, act with discipline, and live with integrity. Your circle will either lift you up or pull you down financially and mentally.

11. "No matter how great the talent or efforts, some things just take time. You can't produce a baby in one month by getting nine women pregnant."

Financial freedom isn't instant. No matter how much you earn or invest, it takes years of steady compounding. Patience is part of the process.

12. "Do not save what is left after spending; instead spend what is left after saving."

This is Buffett's way of saying: *pay yourself first*. Treat savings and investing as non-negotiable. Build your financial freedom fund before you buy luxuries.

Buffett's wisdom proves that wealth isn't built on luck or genius — it's built on discipline, patience, and the right mindset.

Dear Reader,

Thank you — truly — for choosing this book and walking with me through its pages. I know you could have picked up countless other books on money, wealth, or investing, but you gave your time and attention to this one. That means more than I can express. My greatest hope is that these words have given you more than knowledge — that they've given you clarity, courage, and a plan you can carry into the rest of your life.

Throughout this journey, we've covered many important truths:

- That financial freedom is not a dream for the lucky few, but a practical path anyone can take if they are disciplined and consistent.

- That money begins with **active income** — through methods like websites, YouTube, digital photography, trading, or freelancing — but it cannot stop there.

- That the true key is forcing a portion of that income into **passive investments** — real estate, dividend stocks, index funds, bonds, savings products, and even carefully managed Bitcoin positions. These are what allow your money to work while you sleep.

- That along the way, you must protect your mindset: avoiding scams, ignoring trolls and toxic people, choosing the right mentors, and surrounding yourself with those who lift you higher.

If you take only one thing from this book, let it be this: **consistency beats intensity.** You don't need to get rich overnight. You don't need to chase every opportunity. You need to start small, keep going, and let time do its magic. Whether it's saving 10% of your income, investing 1–2% monthly into Bitcoin, reinvesting dividends, or slowly growing a real estate portfolio — every small, steady action multiplies in the years to come.

I began this book by telling you that poverty is hard, and financial freedom is also hard. The difference is that one leaves you trapped, while the other sets you free. The choice, now, is in your hands.

So I leave you with a challenge: **Start today.** Not tomorrow, not next year, not "when the time feels right." Pick one step, no matter how small — and take it. Open the account. Write the first blog post. Buy the first stock. Deposit the first $100. That tiny decision will grow roots that can change your entire future.

Thank you again for reading. I wish you wisdom, courage, discipline, and patience on your journey. Financial freedom is not just possible for you — it is waiting for you. Now it's your turn to claim it.

With gratitude,
Vahid Chaychi

Made in the USA
Columbia, SC
22 September 2025

62318542R00127